A LIFE SPENT LISTENING

A LIFE SPENT
LISTENING

HASSAN KHALILI, PhD

BREAKWATER
P.O. Box 2188, St. John's, NL, Canada, A1C 6E6
www.breakwaterbooks.com

A CIP catalogue record for this book is available from Library and Archives Canada.

We acknowledge the support of the Canada Council for the Arts. We acknowledge the financial support of the Government of Canada and the Government of Newfoundland and Labrador through the Department of Tourism, Culture, Industry and Innovation for our publishing activities. PRINTED AND BOUND IN CANADA.

Canada Council   Conseil des arts
for the Arts   du Canada

Breakwater Books is committed to choosing papers and materials for our books that help to protect our environment. To this end, this book is printed on a recycled paper that is certified by the Forest Stewardship Council®.

*To the people who have talked and
shared their stories with me. To my beautiful family
and friends. To my ancient, beloved, Persian
homeland and my home—the beautiful province of
Newfoundland and Labrador.*

The good life is a process,
not a state of being.
It is a direction,
not a destination.

CARL ROGERS (1902–1987)

i

FINDING MY PLACE IN LIFE

JACKASSES, BRAIN FARTS, AND A MAGIC SCREWDRIVER

♪♪♪

TUNE-UPS FOR RELATIONSHIPS

iv

THE CONTENTMENT CAKE

DISCLAIMER: In order to illustrate and explain my point, I have mentioned some patients/clients. These are illustrative cases and do not represent any particular individuals. Patient confidentiality is of the utmost importance, and the right to privacy has been respected.

1

Finding My Place
in Life

FINDING THE DELICIOUS MOMENTS OF LIFE

I COME FROM a city in the middle of a desert.

In the summertime, the temperature can easily surpass forty-five degrees Celsius. When I was a young boy and the temperature climbed to those heights, having any kind of fun seemed out of the question. It was just too hot. Even if it wasn't too hot, there wasn't much for kids to do—this was long before the concept of "child-friendly" pursuits came into existence.

I was raised in Qom, Iran, south of Tehran. Although Qom has grown into a thriving industrial city of 1.3 million people today, it was the size of St. John's, Newfoundland, in my youth. This was before the Iranian Revolution, which transformed Iran from a secular state to one governed by religious leaders. But even in my youth, Qom was a holy city and the centre of Shi'a Muslim scholarship. The running joke was that Qom had one export, mullah, and one import—the dead. Funerals were so common that every day, I might see two or three on my way to and from school. Death ceased to hold drama and became part of the scenery.

However, it is neither the scorching heat nor the constant funeral atmosphere that I think of when I remember my childhood. Even in the most hostile environments, kids will always find ways to entertain themselves and enjoy their lives. And as a child, I found something that has always stayed with me.

My road to absolute pleasure was through cream puffs.

There were a lot of small shops in my city that huddled together in covered alleys to afford a bit of protection against the blistering sun. These alleys didn't always smell so nice in the heat of the day, and they could look a little scary because they were so dark and closed in. But one was different. It contained a bakery, and the rich, sweet aroma coming from that bakery would lure me into that alley as if I was attached to a fishing line.

Every day, Haj Ali got up before sunrise for his morning Muslim prayer, then walked to his bakery—a one-storey, dome-shaped, mud-brick building. There, he would create a delicate pastry using local flour, milk, and eggs, and fill it with the freshest, creamiest filling. By eight or nine in the morning, his heavenly cream puffs were ready for sale, displayed alongside other treats on a front-facing wooden shelf. But because there were no coolers or refrigerators to store leftovers, the pastries were available only in limited numbers.

They were my favourite treat. Many days, I was the first to arrive at the shop.

People in North America talk about their first teenage kiss and how delicious it was. This did not mean much to me, as we grew up not being allowed to date. But what people describe as their first magical kiss—that measure of softness, deliciousness, and pleasure—is the feeling that I experienced with each of Haj Ali's cream puffs.

To this day, I remember the heavenly taste of the cream puffs from that shop. I search out cream puffs wherever I go, trying to find one as magical as those made by Haj Ali, the king of cream puffs. The thought of cream puffs, the memory of their smell and taste, can take me to heaven. It is a heaven I have created for myself.

Life sometimes can become rough, unfair, and painful. However, the cream puff world I created in my mind is one of absolute joy. It belongs to me and the little guy inside me. I taught myself to open up a beautiful place in my brain where these cream puffs could live forever. Over the years, I've continued to build this place, slowly adding memorable scenery, warm conversations, beautiful smiles, close friendships, funny jokes, favourite smells and tastes, comforting touches—anything that brings me joy.

As more and more of my mind is taken up with the beauty of this temple I have created, there is increasingly less space for all the negative emotions and ugly images and memories I have experienced. I have chosen to deliberately jettison them to make space for all the "cream puff moments" in my life.

However, this is not quite enough to content me. I want to share my journey, and I want everyone to be able to make their own lives better by building their own "cream puff world"—a world that lifts the weight of the terrible things that happen to all of us. The purpose of creating such interior worlds is to help people to cope and maybe even to find joy in life.

Too often, we allow ourselves to be caught up in the negative. It's a downward spiral, but we can turn it around. This book is a guide for doing that. It is based on many years of treating patients both privately and in a hospital setting. I use examples from my practice and specific tools I have developed over the years to help my patients not only cope with problems but defeat them altogether. Some problems need gentle handling. Some are more receptive to a firmer, more direct approach. I use whatever method is necessary.

I have never just spoken to my patients. I have always listened as well, and there, perhaps, is where the best of my own personal path towards enlightenment has taken place—that and the physical journeys I have taken with my friends (this is something I am keen to share.) So this book is about me as much as it is about what I've learned from and with my patients. It includes my "life list," my travels, even stories about making an ass of myself.

I will introduce you to the Khalili Grid, a system that I devised many years ago to help my patients achieve a state of contentment and balance. I will teach you about the importance of knowing where to tap and introduce you to my quest for the golden screwdriver.

Whether it's sharing the lessons I've learned from my patients or those I've drawn from my travels, my goal is to take the reader on a fun and enlightening journey.

Because everyone deserves some delicious cream puffs in their life.

FOLLOWING DREAMS

IN THE MOVIE, *The Bucket List*, two terminally ill men set out on a quest to do all the things that they had always dreamed of doing, before they "kicked the bucket." I believe everyone should have such a list.

Imagining what you can do with your life gives it meaning. However, we certainly should not wait until we are staring death in the face before we set out to reach our goals. A list of things we would like to accomplish in life—which sounds much more positive than a bucket list—should be with us always.

Think of it as a "life list" rather than a bucket list. It is not a list of what you want to accomplish before you die; it is what you want to accomplish in your life.

Although I did not realize it at the time, I started building my list when I was very young. Back then I thought I was just dreaming, letting my imagination off the leash to wander wherever it wanted to go. It ended up going an awfully long way.

Every year of my youth, I spent at least four months in Aveh, a village of approximately thirty-five hundred people that was mostly owned by the Khalili family. This is where my family's farms and pomegranate orchards were located. My cousins, whose families also owned pomegranate orchards, came to stay with us for the summer months. There were dozens of us, boys and girls playing together in a wide expanse of open space, zigzagging among the ten-foot-tall pomegranate trees with their lush, round fruits hanging within reach.

Life was simple. There was no electricity, no television, no internet, no fridge, no stove, no intrusions from the outside world except the few stations that our battery-operated radio picked up. We spent our days hunting scorpions, chasing rabbits and small coyotes, riding jackasses, and eating fruit. It was a beautiful time.

But it was hot. The sun beamed down all day and there was little rain. Imagine how hot it got in the small mud and mud-brick houses, when the temperature often climbed above forty degrees Celsius and never dropped below thirty. To get any sleep at all, we brought portable beds up onto the rooftops, which were covered in beautiful Persian rugs. It was a bit cooler up there, and sometimes there might be a breeze. I remember the smell of the farm animals and the freshness of the air in the moonlight. I remember how the stars seemed so close I was sure I could touch them. I remember our dog, Jooli, who always slept next to us.

On the rooftop, surrounded by beloved family, you could chat quietly as you stared at the stars and drifted off to sleep, or you could let your mind soar.

This is where my imagination took flight. I still recall, very clearly, the dreams and wishes I formulated during those years. I wanted to visit God, the creator of all men. I wanted to know if other boys like me looked at stars, and I wanted to talk to them. I wanted to know where my father was. I knew he had died, but I wanted to see heaven, where I knew he was, and not just talk about it. I had learned about a special, magical pomegranate that was the fruit from heaven, capable of curing all illness and banishing all pain. I wanted to find it—in fact, I tested thousands of pomegranates from thousands of trees in the family orchard. This orchard covered about twenty-five hectares and contained many different varieties. And I ran from tree to tree, taking a single bite of fruit, searching for it. Those were my earliest dreams.

As I got older, my dreams changed. I learned to read, and the world opened up to me as I travelled in my imagination with Gulliver, Ali Baba, Hercules, the women of the Amazon, the Persian hero Rostam, and many more. I was using my imagination and listening to others use theirs.

Later still, I was old enough to go to the movies, and my world of the imagination expanded even more. I went to see *Twenty Thousand Leagues under the Sea* repeatedly. I was also fascinated by the American Wild West as it was portrayed in the movies. I especially liked John Wayne, and I wanted to know what he was really saying, not what the dubbed Persian version said he was saying.

This led to the first entry on my life list. I decided I wanted to learn how to speak English. It was not easy. I was able to read elementary English books, nursery rhymes like "Pat-a-cake, pat-a-cake." In high school and in the summer, I went to an English class offered by the Iranian-American society. It was hard, but I was motivated by my dream and my nascent life list.

My other dream was to help people—everyone, of course, but mostly my family and friends. So I listened to them very carefully to see what they needed; this made me extremely popular. I got invited everywhere because I had the desire and the skill to hear what people were saying. I suppose I was a psychotherapist from an early age, even though that was not my specific dream. I did dream of getting my doctorate, and that became so much a part of me that when I defended my dissertation and my committee welcomed me to the "PhD club," I felt as if I had belonged to it for years.

I wonder how much I would have accomplished without those early dreams—those early list entries I compiled before the term "bucket list" had even been invented.

A life list gives you something to look forward to and something to work towards, and it must evolve constantly to meet your ever-changing needs. You cannot just get to the end of a finite list and say "done." That would defeat the purpose.

Not everyone believes such a list is a good thing. Some say it gives you tunnel vision—that you become so focused on a particular goal that you miss the opportunities all around you. They contend that high expectations can sabotage you and leave you worse off than before, that you will end up feeling obligated and then regretful, that your ambitions will turn you into nothing but a tourist and limit you and what you can do.

I disagree. I encourage my patients to have a life list because I believe in it, and here is why: it keeps you in touch with your goals. It gets you in touch with your values, helps you to enjoy life, and keeps track of your peak experiences. It gives you purpose and direction, pushing you forward and keeping you focused. It helps you to discover, explore, and learn. And it enriches your memories and makes life more meaningful if you include others and contribute to society.

However, a life list should not be a "must-do" list; rather, it should help give life direction and purpose. It should not be narcissistic but connect us to something larger by including others.

Everyone has dreams and everyone should have something to look forward to. The dreams do not have to be complicated, but we must figure out what they are. Sometimes I suggest to my patients they have a look at the Khalili Grid (which you will discover in a few chapters). They will see a picture of themselves, their family, their neighbourhood, and their work, and then envision how to make these four components come together better.

What is on my life list now? Well, it is always changing, as it should. Except for travelling the Silk Road in the footsteps of my Persian ancestors, which I did in 2017, many of the items on my list were developed in consultation with my hiking buddies. Together we have planned and carried out trips all over the world. We hiked up to Machu Picchu in Peru in 2007; we climbed Mount Kilimanjaro in Tanzania in 2010; we visited and hiked in Antarctica in 2012; and we walked the Camino de Santiago in Spain in 2014.

I have experienced incredible adventures with this shared list, and it has offered me other advantages. Since I want to continue to enjoy these experiences, I am encouraged to remain in shape. I get up at five o'clock every morning to go to the gym, so I can continue to be fit enough to see the world on foot with my friends. I have other things on my list besides hiking with my buddies.

Khalili's List

- *Learn Spanish.*
- *Share my experiences and wisdom with others (hence this book).*
- *Go on many more hikes.*
- *Invent a magic screwdriver (more about that later).*
- *See my grandchildren grow up and be happy, as my children are now.*
- *Watch my profession grow and prevent more mental health problems.*

Some things on my list are small. Some are larger. The list will change as I go along. That is the way it should be. I have a long way to go yet!

And maybe, someday, I might even find that magic pomegranate.

THE JOURNEY FROM THERE TO HERE

FOR FOUR DECADES, I have been a Canadian front-line community psychologist in St. John's—North America's easternmost city. It's a very long way from Iran, and the route to my professional designation was not exactly straightforward.

I got my first degree in counselling children at the Teacher Training University in my home country of Iran. But I quickly discovered I did not have the patience to work with children, so I returned to the family farm and worked in agribusiness. I was good at it, but I did not excel. I decided to go to the United States and get my Master of Business Administration (MBA) to help me improve.

This was in the 1970s. For some years, Iran had been undergoing what the Iranian Imperial Government called the "White Revolution," which involved changes towards modernization and westernization. Not everyone supported these changes, however. There was opposition from left-wing and religious groups.

While I was studying for my MBA in Kansas, the opposition forces gained strength and in 1978, the Revolution began, leading to the establishment of the Islamic Republic of Iran. Many people believed that the new regime would improve their financial, social, and political situation, but there was considerable turmoil. My family advised me to wait a bit longer before coming home. I waited. Then a group of Islamic Iranian students took over the American Embassy in Tehran and took the staff hostage. This created problems for Iranian students like me in the United States (eventually I would choose to move to Canada). The turmoil continued, and then a war between Iran and Iraq went on for eight years. Hundreds of thousands of people were killed and displaced from both sides. These events shifted my life direction, though it took several years for me to accept the difficult emotional reality that I would never move back to the homeland I loved— and still love—dearly.

While I was waiting for the turmoil to ease, I finished my MBA and also a Master's in counselling and started the doctoral program at the University of Iowa. Since a doctorate in business seemed useful only for an academic career, I returned to my first love—psychology. This time I studied adult counselling.

It was during my early studies in the United States that I discovered another love—a woman named Clarines. We met shortly after I arrived in Kansas to attend Emporia State University. She had come from Colombia to study English and French.

Clarines worked in the English language lab, and I was often there. When she saw my concentration waning, she would jolt me back to the task at hand. We became very close friends. We were both missing our faraway families but had no family in Kansas. We spent time walking, talking, and sharing meals. Eventually we became so close that we thought of each other as family.

We both intended to return to our home countries, and so had no plans of being together into the future. We came from two extremely different cultures, languages, and religions. She was South American, Spanish-speaking, and Roman Catholic; I was a Persian-speaking Iranian and had grown up as Shiite Muslim. But our friendship was strong. The little boy and little girl inside us liked each other and wanted to be friends. Nobody else really understood that.

Clarines finished her Master's in information management, got a good job with the Colombian oil industry, and went back home. It was very hard on both of us, but we understood the situation.

We kept in touch by letter and sometimes telephone (this was long before the internet). Neither of us could let go of our friendship and the love we had for each other. Finally, she decided that she could not let me go and came back to the United States. We wanted to be together, to create a home and start a family. And so, more than forty years ago, I married my best buddy.

Clarines and I have built a beautiful life in Canada with two children, Donnamarie and Sammy. Donnamarie is now married to Alistair, a genuine, resourceful human being, and they live right next door to us. Sammy is further away, living and working in the United States. He is married to Lindsay, who is a beautiful, kind person, and they have three children: Nico, Lucas, and Sofia. Our children are truly global citizens. They are Newfoundlanders and Canadians, Iranians, and Colombians.

MY PATIENTS AND ME

I CHOSE A career in psychology because I wanted to make a difference in people's lives.

Why do my patients come to see me and what do I do to help them?

Most people—not all, but most—come to see me because of problems with one of the following: mental health and coping issues; dealing with relationships, both with themselves and with others; identifying the issue and what needs to be assessed; decision making; shedding what I call "emotional fat"; or dealing with stress, loss, or fear.

My patients do not know me as a person, only as a professional—their psychologist. They come to see me in the hopes that I will be able to help them. That is my job: identifying the issue and helping them cope or resolve the problem. Many times, they don't really know what they are looking for.

"I don't know" is often one of the first things I hear. People use this phrase as a coping strategy—if they do not know what the issue is, then they do not have to deal with it. Yet they have come to me for help and expect results, so I must figure out the problem before anything else. In that very first session, I have one hour to establish what needs to be done and how to do it. I do not let my patient leave without a plan.

There are many ways to get past those "I don't know" responses and to figure out what is wrong. I usually tell my patients that I am going to turn on three "cameras."

The first is a clinical/chemical camera. It takes a picture of the client's medical history, their family's medical history, their blood test results, medications, physical injuries, and anything physical that might affect them mentally.

The second takes a photograph of their behaviour: what they do, or do not do, that causes problems. These patterns include sleep habits, work habits, exercise, diet, and social life.

The third takes a snapshot of their mental habits: their values, belief system, and way of thinking, as well as their upbringing and any past issues they may have had.

The more efficient I am at asking the right questions—at getting a complete picture—the more quickly we can arrive at the right answers and figure out what our roles are, what needs to be done and how to do it. It is important to establish this as soon as possible.

A woman visited me who was trying to cope with the death of her only child. One of the questions I asked her was what she had done with the ashes. I learned that she kept them on a shelf in her bedroom, even though her son had asked her to spread them. She felt that if she followed his wishes, she would not have him anymore, that he would truly be gone. But she did not have him anyway. We had the answer to her problem and a plan.

Generally, after the initial consultation, we have a strategy for moving forward. From there, it usually takes four or five sessions to deal with an issue. If it is resolved, then we are done.

That's the perfect scenario. However, life does not always work this way. Some clients have chronic issues, and I see them over longer periods of time. For them, therapy is like medication: they need it in order to maintain their mental health.

Sometimes a patient will have many issues, but because I am in private practice, we can only concentrate on one because of financial constraints. At other times, I discover they do not need a clinical psychologist. In these cases, I recommend an addiction program or grief program. I try to make sure they get the most appropriate care for their needs.

Sometimes, however, I have patients who are not really committed to therapy. They are just kicking my tires, and I cannot do much for them except present some options. And over the course of my career there have been occasional situations when a client and I just have not connected. Either they do not like me or vice versa. In cases like these, I recommended an alternate psychologist.

Sometimes I have the opposite problem: patients who no longer need me want to continue their treatment because they have formed a connection with me. It is a constant challenge to maintain professional relationship boundaries and remind them, and me too sometimes, that we are not friends.

These are all challenges. However, I also owe it to myself to enjoy what I do and use what I have learned over the years. As with any positive relationship, communication is paramount. I am clear with my patients about what I am able (or not able) to do, and what my expectation is of them. Therapy is a two-way street, and clients have to be present and take part in their own treatment. They need to be responsible for their own wellness.

It brings me a lot of joy to see my patients get better. It is not just what they say (that is just good for the ego!); it is seeing them improve and knowing that I have played a part in helping them by doing the best job I can.

I make a living doing something I really love. For this, I am one of the fortunate ones.

THE KHALILI GRID

ABOUT TWENTY-FIVE years ago, a polite, gentle, and very wealthy man came to see me for a consultation. He had all the qualities that would make for a happy person; however, he was not a happy or healthy man. His third marriage was breaking up and he had suffered a couple of heart attacks. It was a morning appointment, and I had a pot of coffee in my office. I offered him a cup, which he accepted. Then he picked up the cup and downed the drink as if it were a shot of tequila.

I was quite surprised and asked him why he drank coffee in such a way. His reply was very offhand.

"Who cares? It's only a coffee."

"But coffee is a way to take a break and talk," I argued.

"I do not have time for that," he said.

I was well on the way to seeing what his problem was.

I have also seen people with the opposite attitude. They party a lot and say, "Life is too short. You must enjoy it."

But their work suffers, their home life suffers, and they have health problems.

One person works too hard. One person parties too hard. They seem to be exact opposites, and yet the result is precisely the same problem.

I have been watching people for a long time. I see incredibly happy people, very depressed people, and all the people in between. Most people fall somewhere in the middle.

When I began my practice, I could not help but wonder why there was such a spread. Why were some at one end of the spectrum and some at the other? I started looking for causes, trying to figure out what it was that made people happy or sad.

I saw people who were wealthy but not healthy, people who were wealthy and healthy but had a difficult home life. I also saw people who had health, wealth, and a good home life, but were still not enjoying life. I wanted to figure out why. There had to be more to it than financial security or the ability to run twenty kilometres or even a solid marriage.

It took me many years to conclude that it was a question of balance. If the balance of our lives is off-kilter, then we are going to be unhappy. What is it we need to balance?

Eventually, I came up with a list. It is remarkably simple. Our lives are ruled by four things:

1. *Health—our physical health, our mental health, our spiritual health, and our cultural health.*

2. *Home—our family, our other relationships, our friendships, and our actual physical home.*

3. *Work—what we do with our days, whether it is simply a job or more of a career, whether our job matches our personality and ability, and whether we like what we do.*

4. *Hobbies and pastimes—what we like to do when we are not working and whether we do enough of whatever it is.*

I thought about this list very carefully, and then I realized that the priority we place on these factors is what matters in life and what makes us happy. We needed to put them in order of importance and recognize that this order might change over time. If we put them in the wrong order, then our lives will be out of balance. I came up with a simple schematic I call the Khalili Grid.

This is what it looks like for people in their middle, working years:

Health - 1	Hobbies - 4
Home - 2	Work - 3

Taking care of your health ranks as number one and always will, because if you ignore your health (mental, physical, or spiritual), maintaining the other three areas will become impossible.

As you get older, physical problems will only get worse if you have not been paying attention to your health all along. I compare running a body to running a car. How long do you expect your car to last if you do not give it regular oil changes and have the brakes and tires checked occasionally? Yet some people expect their body to just keep going and going, no matter how hard they abuse it. It won't. We need to pay attention to diet, exercise, and sleep. If we have chronic health issues, this diligent care is even more important.

Of course, health is not just physical, even though we often think of it that way. We must devote the same attention to our emotional, mental, and spiritual health. If these things are not in order, tuned up, and ready to hit the highway, how are we going to successfully navigate our way through home, work, and hobbies?

The second most important factor is home—by which I mean the place where we experience our intimate relationships. Our relationships with other people are the most momentous things we have outside our own health. In a way, this is like number one. Our relationships must be healthy as well. We need to look forward to coming home at night (or whenever we get off work) and to do that, we must nurture our relationships with others.

Marriages need tune-ups, just like bodies and cars. You cannot neglect them any more than you can neglect your health without suffering the consequences. I frequently meet people who have "bad" kids. At least that is what they say, but often these kids are not bad at all. The problem is simply that they are not being given enough time by their parents.

My coffee-drinking patient was neglecting both these crucial quadrants. That is why he had experienced two heart attacks and was struggling in his relationship with his third wife. His life was completely out of balance because he did not recognize that for a well-balanced life, work should be the third priority.

We are supposed to work as a means of making a living. However, for too many people, work becomes much more than that. They sacrifice their health, their home life, and their hobbies to work. But as so many end-of-life caregivers can attest, no one at the end of their life ever complained, "I wish I'd worked more and spent less time with my family." Work is a part of our lives, and it is an important part of our lives. But it is not life itself. Do not make it number one.

The final part of the Khalili Grid is hobbies. Most people—

aside from those who spend long hours in the basement playing with their Xbox—badly neglect this. Yet we all need to spend time doing things we enjoy. While many of us enjoy our work, we need something else that we do simply for pleasure. We need to relax, and we need to be stimulated in different ways.

As we grow older, we rely on these hobbies more and more. After we retire, this category moves up to the number three position. Yet many people are completely unprepared for retirement and dread the thought of those empty days. Too many people fall into a depression or even die soon after they retire because they simply have nothing to replace work. They have lost their purpose.

I must make a confession here. Although I am past the traditional retirement age, one reason I am still working is that I have not developed the hobby side of life to the extent that it can take over completely from work. So I too am still working on getting the balance right.

Balance is what it is all about. Sometimes I say to patients who are struggling, "Come, let's check the Khalili Grid." We see if they are neglecting one of the four corners or if they are putting too much emphasis on a particular quadrant. After we assess this, then we can create a formal plan that will return life to a balanced state.

Working too much is going to have a terrible effect on your relationships and hobbies. Spending too much time in bars with friends is going to have a terrible effect on your work and health (and pocketbook), and so on.

Years of observation and thoughtful reflection have convinced me that if you make sure you balance the four quadrants on the Khalili Grid, you can have a happy life.

PSYCHOTHERAPY VS. COUNSELLING

LIKE MANY PROFESSIONS, psychology uses certain terms that mean specific things. Over the years, however, the public has interpreted some of these terms in new ways. Did you know that the word "hysteria" used to refer to the irrational behaviour of women specifically, and that mediaeval doctors attributed this to women having a uterus? Did you know that "insanity" is no longer considered a medical diagnosis, even though it is still used in legal cases in the United States? Words like "certifiable" and "psycho" are now just catch-all synonyms for "crazy," which is another word we do not use in the mental health field.

So it is not surprising that people see little to distinguish between the terms "counselling" and "psychotherapy." People refer to someone in counselling or in therapy as if they were the same thing. But they are not actually the same thing and should not be used interchangeably.

In practice, counselling is recommended for specific issues and situations. These include grief, conflict, addiction, and certain specific behaviours. Counselling usually takes place over a limited number of sessions and does not usually last more than a few weeks or months. It is used to help people get over a bump or around an obstacle in their journey through life. Often, it simply involves passing on information.

Psychotherapy, on the other hand, usually goes deeper into issues for a much longer period. The American Psychological Association defines psychotherapy as the "informed and intentional application of clinical methods and interpersonal stances derived from established psychological principles for the purpose of assisting people to modify their behaviors, cognitions, emotions and/or other personal characteristics in directions that the participants deem desirable."

That's a mouthful to say, "here's what we do to help people get better."

The phrase "interpersonal stances" is critical to this definition because it recognizes the important role of the quality of the therapeutic relationship in patient outcomes. In other words, if the patient and the therapist do not get along, there is a greater chance of the psychotherapy failing, and if they have a good relationship, there is a greater chance of the psychotherapy succeeding.

That is one of the reasons psychotherapists must have much more training than counsellors. Psychotherapy is much more taxing for the therapist. In my work, I do both counselling and psychotherapy. Since I work in private practice (not in the public health-care system, which is covered by provincial health care), I have to be mindful of my patients' financial situation, so I must use my time wisely.

Patients who are resistant, who have pre-treatment factors like functional impairments or comorbidity (where a patient has more than one health condition), or who have a character and personality disorder do not do well in a limited structure where they can only afford treatment for a little while.

For these reasons, it is extremely important for me to identify related patient factors (aspects of the patient's life and health that can affect the results of therapy) and to be honest in telling them what I can and cannot do. That can be difficult because it feels as though the more I do my job, the more I realize how much I do not know.

I recently saw a fifty-year-old businessman. He owns a mostly seasonal business, which operates from April to December. During that time, he works seven days a week and puts in long hours. To keep himself going, he started smoking cigarettes and pot. Eventually, he moved up to cocaine and developed a habit that cost him several thousand dollars a week. He also had symptoms of compulsive, but not full, obsessive-compulsive disorder (OCD).

His wife was worried about him, and he was willing to commit to a few hours of counselling to satisfy her wish for him to receive treatment. However, he had no intention of quitting his drug habit or slowing down his work schedule.

In the first half of our session, I realized that although he was a good man, he had many past and present issues, and his addiction and compulsivity were quite severe. He needed an inpatient drug addiction program and a clear treatment plan. He was a good candidate for psychotherapy.

I used the Khalili Grid to show him where the problem spots were: health issues, work issues, and bad habits. I told him that if we did not develop a comprehensive plan, and he depended on a few sessions of counselling, the outcome would probably be poor and neither his health nor his situation would improve. In fact, it might even get worse, considering how much he was spending on his cocaine addiction. His wife came in with him to draw up a plan. If he follows it, I have confidence that it will be effective.

If a person stays long enough in psychotherapy with a trained psychotherapist, then the outcome can be incredibly positive. But the patient factor needs to be fully considered when we plan out a course of treatment.

The other significant issue in psychotherapy is the relationship between the therapist and the patient. The therapist must be able to project warmth, respect, emotional communication, security, and hope, and be able to manage counter-transference, which at its simplest is a therapist's emotional entanglement with a patient. If a patient brings up a past issue at the therapist's prodding, the therapist must be prepared to expend the time, energy, and skills needed to deal with that issue.

It can be exceedingly difficult to maintain a professional balance in a relationship with a patient. I have learned this when my relationship with a patient is ruptured, whether through the passage of time, misunderstandings, the demands of life, or administrative, ethical, or legal issues. It is crucial to repair that relationship. Every case is different.

I recall helping a man who was a few years younger than me. He was a lonely man with limited experience of friendship. I knew that in his heart he considered me his friend. I explained to him several times that we had a professional/therapy relationship only, but it meant more to him than that. It took a lot of skill for me to remain a therapist and not become a buddy for this man.

In another case, I helped a woman through her second and third pregnancies because she had postpartum depression after her first one. In addition to my work with the woman, I also came to know her husband. Her postpartum depression was significantly reduced with these two pregnancies. When she became pregnant again, she asked me to stand as godfather for her fourth child. I had to explain to her, with as much respect and empathy as I could, that this would be stepping over the line. Unfortunately, she did not accept my refusal, and this broke our therapist/patient relationship.

But there are times when my being present at a personal event is part of the therapy. Each instance must be considered individually. I have to evaluate the benefit to my patient and whether any confidentiality or ethics lines would be crossed.

In one instance, I helped a woman in her late sixties deal with her relationship with her mother, who was in her nineties. The mother had been harsh and hurtful to my patient, who was her oldest child. She blamed the daughter for ruining her life because it was her pregnancy that had forced her to marry my patient's father. I am pleased to say the woman's psychotherapy was successful and wrapped up after about a year.

Four years later, she called and asked me to attend her mother's wake and I did. This extra step on my part helped my former patient a great deal. She told me at the funeral how satisfied she was to be at peace with her mother when she died. My presence there was a kind of closure for her.

Another time, I ended up at the wedding of a philanderer whom I had helped to figure out how to be faithful to a woman.

Again, it is a question of benefit—will the patient benefit from my involvement in their life, or will it distract from their well-being? Maintaining a professional distance can be difficult, especially in cases where the therapy relationship has lasted for years or decades. It is impossible not to form human attachments over such a long period of time. However, I work hard to ensure that my human connection to a patient never overrides my dedication to their benefit.

Being a psychotherapist is not an easy task. You do not just perform and stop. It is more of a journey you travel with different people. Sometimes your relationship with your patient changes. That is the beauty of my life. It is always an adventure, and the people in it make it so much richer.

UNDERSTANDING PERSONALITY

C ARVED IN STONE on the Temple of Apollo in Delphi, which was built in the sixth century BCE, are the words "know thyself." Socrates, Plato, and most of the philosophers who followed them, heartily endorsed this sentiment, which probably dates back much further than those ancient times. The admonishment to understand one's own personality is still as relevant today as it was then.

The word personality is derived from the Latin *personalitatum*, which means "the quality of being a person."

What exactly do we mean when we talk about a person's personality? Sometimes we use it dismissively, as a kind of code for "what did you expect?" A person's behaviour is explained away as "just their personality," especially if they do something disappointing or less than admirable. We have expectations of how someone will act or react based on what we believe to be true about their personality. However, there is more to personality than that, and we need to understand its components.

We begin life with the basic structure of our personality, and over time as we grow and have various experiences, our personality develops with us. Much goes into the building of a personality: character, traits, drive, and a whole host of other factors.

Character is made up of the mental and moral qualities we possess. These include honesty, integrity, patience, and stability—or, of course, the opposite of these things. A person of strong character has these positive features in their makeup. A person of weak character does not.

Traits are distinguishing qualities that are mostly determined by genetics. Agreeableness, calmness, and composure, for example, are components of our personality that we have no more control over than the colour of our eyes or how tall we are. We can wear coloured contacts or hold our tongue when our temper flares, but we cannot change the underlying trait.

Drive is our motivation—our compulsion (or lack thereof) to move forward.

I think of personality as like the house we live in. Some parts of it are already constructed when we move in, and other parts we must design and decorate ourselves. We need to know it well, if only so we can deal with any problems that arise. If there is a leak in the attic, you do not want to waste time looking for problems in the basement. The whole main floor could be ruined by the time you realize where the trouble lies.

If you know your own personality, you can keep the more negative parts of it in check. For example, I am too caring. That does not sound like a problem, does it? But it is. I end up spending far too long and going out of my way for people who do not really need me to do so. I am the guy who will spend ages sending picture after picture of a wedding to people who did not attend, just so they will not miss out. But most of them do not want all those pictures clogging up their inboxes and phones. I must remember that and stop myself from getting carried away. Similarly, I put in hours and hours of unpaid work so my patients get the best care possible, and that adversely affects other areas of my life.

This is a personality trait I watch out for constantly and try to keep in check.

The main function of a personality is to help us form relationships, adjust to the world, and be content and happy. When we meet someone, we assess their personality and look for ways to make a connection with them. It's one of the ways that society works.

This is also something I do in my work. I assess the parameters of my patients' personalities, looking for a way to connect. I use certain criteria: how they perceive their work, needs, finances, and so on; how they understand and manage their emotions; how they relate to others; and how they manage their impulses.

Through my training and ongoing professional development, I have learned to assess personalities and to diagnose various mental disorders based on the *Diagnostic and Statistical Manual of Mental Disorders*, 5th edition (*DSM-5*).[1] This assessment helps me to get a handle on what kind of personality a new patient has.

When I discover that a patient might have a personality disorder, I try to help them fix whatever the problem might be— whether a room needs repainting or the plumbing needs updating. Of course, not everyone has a personality disorder, or even some of the symptoms of a personality disorder. Many people have behavioural problems and struggle to maintain good relationships with others.

When we understand our personality, we understand our behaviour, and when we understand our behaviour, we can correct it. Notice that I am talking about correcting our own behaviour. I never say, "I corrected my patients' behaviour for them."

A few years ago, I saw a married couple because the husband wanted out of the marriage for no apparent reason. His problem was impulsivity, and he felt that life would be better if he left his wife, even though he had no real idea what he would do if he carried through with his impulse. I helped him break down the factors that made him feel this way and he stayed with his wife,

---

[1] The *Diagnostic and Statistical Manual of Mental Disorders*, 5th edition (*DSM-5*), published by the American Psychiatric Association, is widely used by everyone from mental health professionals to policy makers.

but he did not stay with her because of me. He stayed with her because he finally understood what he was doing and what it would mean. He had learned to know himself and understand his personality.

KNOWING WHERE TO TAP

I GOOGLED "KNOWING where to tap" and got 139,000,000 hits. It's a story about the difference between just doing something and actually knowing what to do. It first appeared in print in England in 1908 and has been retold countless times— maybe even more than 139,000,000 times!

Here is the version I first heard:

> The main machine in a factory broke down and the manager called in an expert. The expert arrived with a hammer in his hand. He started tapping on different parts of the machine and listening to the sound it made. Then on one part he started tapping more and more, and as a result the machine started working. The next day the manager received a bill for one thousand dollars. He became upset, called the expert, and said, "You are charging me a thousand dollars for a few taps?! You must itemize your bill." The next day the manager received the following bill:
>
> Tapping: $20
>
> Knowing where to tap: $980
>
> The bill was high not because the expert spent a few minutes tapping the machine, but because he had the skill to understand how the machine worked and what needed repairing.

In my work, I have seen thousands of people whose mental health or relationships are not working, and they come to me to fix whatever is wrong. At times, I see myself with a hammer in my hand, tapping on them, looking for the right spot, and sometimes that spot can be very difficult to find. It makes my job remarkably interesting. I call that sweet spot—the right place to tap—insight. Insight into those behaviours and habits that are the cause of the problem; insight into those belief systems and mental habits that are behind those feelings and behaviours. The spot you tap to get the whole machine running properly again.

I once had a patient whom I had been treating for twenty years. He was steadily building his career, moving into higher and higher positions at work. Every time he got a new job, he came to me, and I taught him how to tap, because every position needed slightly different skills. Finding the right place to tap may be as simple as figuring out how to introduce yourself to someone— this is a tap that you need to know to succeed both socially and in business.

He is now at the very top of his field, but for a long time he had one problem that we could not resolve, no matter how well we dealt with everything else. He weighed 250 pounds, and both my patient and his family doctor were worried about the impact of his obesity on his health. However, I could not seem to help him balance his diet and exercise. No matter how hard I tried, I could not find the right place to tap—to activate the insight he needed to get to a healthier weight. Then, when he was in his fifties, he developed diabetes and was put on four or five different medications. He hated that reliance on medication, and I had finally been shown the right place to tap. I pointed out to him that if he wanted to get rid of the pills, he had to diet and exercise.

He was finally given a solid reason—the right tap—to do what he needed to do.

When we truly develop insight and are committed to correcting a problem, it becomes solvable. We know where to tap. This skill was not automatically granted to me when I received my doctorate. You can have a degree and still have no idea what to do. I learned how to guide people towards insight by truly hearing what they had to say and then responding—by putting my ear to the machine and listening for the clanging noise that indicates where I should use my little hammer.

Many years ago, my mother came to visit me. I had been working in my field for some time and she was curious about it and asked me what I did for a living. I said, "I am a psychologist." She said, "I know that!" She was clearly looking for something more. "I talk to people," I said. She gave me that look that all mothers can command when they think their children are being obtuse in some way—you know the one I mean. And then she said, "Really. But what do you *do?*"

I should have told her I spent the day tapping.

THE MEANING OF LIFE? GIVING LIFE MEANING

I HAVE A friend whose family is stable and financially comfortable and, as far as I can remember, has no history of depression. He is a few years younger than me, so I was surprised when, a while ago, I asked him what he was looking forward to and he replied, "Dying."

Where had that come from?

He really felt there was no point to life. Some people are not as honest as he is, but many feel that life has no meaning.

American psychologist Clara Hill said, "Almost every problem that's brought into therapy is implicitly about the meaning of life." Largely I agree with her, because that has been my experience with my patients as well. But there is a problem with that, because psychologists do not know the meaning of life. Neither do psychiatrists, and they are not alone in this. Scientists, philosophers, religious leaders, bartenders, your mother. They don't know the meaning of life either. (I know that is hard to believe about your mother, but it is true). We may believe we know. We may have almost completely convinced ourselves that we know, but we do not know. We are incapable of knowing. So we cannot hand over the answer to our patients, no matter how much we wish we could.

Yet we cannot be like my pessimistic friend and simply look forward to dying. That is no way to live. So, again, what can we do?

Dr. Irvin D. Yalom, an American existential psychiatrist, holds that life is inherently random and meaningless. Tori DeAngelis explains the consequence of this randomness, which is that "humans must create their own sense of meaning."[2] As you engage fully in life, activities, and people, you are drawn to a life that nourishes you.

That sounds like a good idea. We are here. Let us make it as pleasant an experience as possible. So how does one create a sense of meaning and a belief in the inherent value of life and living?

I think we can do that through certain habits, activities, and patterns of thinking. I believe they can be learned.

The mother of one of my closest friends is ninety years old. She is a retired teacher who has lost two husbands, but she has never lost her love for life. She has a lot to teach people about the

[2] DeAngelis, Tori. "In search of meaning." APA *Monitor on Psychology*, October 2018. Online at https://www.apa.org/monitor/2018/10/cover-search-meaning.

meaning of life, and I have watched her carefully over the years to see what it is she does to maintain that *joie de vivre*. This is what I realized about her: she is regularly active in her community. Whether it involves her church, her faith, her family, or her friends, she never misses an opportunity to participate in whatever is going on around her. She eats well, she goes for walks, and she makes sure she gets the proper amount of sleep. She balances her private time and the time she spends with others, never tipping too much one way or another. She believes in a higher power (which certainly seems to help, although no one knows why). She avoids negativity. She reads and she bakes (without a doubt she makes the best tea biscuits in the world; if she made cream puffs, I bet they would be the best in the world, too); she cooks and she travels.

In other words, she always seems to be doing, is always engaged in one thing or another, and is always learning. She is creating her own meaning, and she is one of the happiest, most content people I know. She loves every minute of her life.

I believe we can all learn to do this—to give life meaning and learn how to savour it—because I think that people like my friend's mother have learned how. They deliberately look on the bright side and have developed the ability to maintain a positive attitude.

We can do this by understanding we have a life and a death, by developing strong relationships, by recognizing the goodness of life, by having a plan that takes in the bigger picture, by accepting our differences, and by learning to appreciate the small things in life.

I recently had a discussion on this very topic with one of my patients. He is in his forties and suffering from lupus. He is waiting for a kidney transplant, and in the meantime, he has to go for dialysis at least three times a week. Each treatment takes about four and a half hours. It is gruelling.

Yet rather than giving up or feeling down, he uses every means possible to hold on to life, including talking to me, even permitting me to write about his case. I asked him, "How did you develop this active and positive attitude?" His answer was a simple one. He said, "My father." My patient's father had the same condition and died at forty-eight. However, despite his medical limitations, he believed that each moment of his life belonged to him. He would "be damned" if he would lose it to despair or negativity.

My patient is so good at keeping up his spirits that I often wonder: who is the helper? Is it me or is it really him?

Does your life make sense *to you?*

No one knows the meaning of life. No one knows the answer. But I believe giving meaning to life is the better path to follow (especially if there are tea biscuits to enjoy along the way).

A COME FROM AWAY WHO STAYED

newfoundland IS AN island in the North Atlantic known for its brutal weather and friendly inhabitants. It has been part of Canada since 1949, but its history goes back much further than that. It was the home of Indigenous inhabitants for millennia before it became Britain's first overseas colony, and it has been home to European fisherfolk for hundreds of years.

In 1985, I was invited to come to St. John's, the capital city on the eastern coast of Newfoundland, for a job interview for the position of senior psychologist at the Waterford Hospital. I immediately fell in love with the beauty of the environment and the congeniality of the people.

I was not here long before I learned a local term used to describe a person who lives here but was not born here: CFA, or Come From Away. These days, this term has become quite well-known as a result of the Broadway play by the same name.

As more time passed, I learned that people were not just divided into Newfoundlanders and Come From Aways. They were also divided into Townies, those who were born and/or lived in St. John's, and the Baymen who lived beyond the borders of the city.

If that was not enough, I then discovered that even within the confines of the city there were east enders and west enders. It presented me with a bit of a dilemma. How on earth was someone like me, who was born in a Persian city in Iran, ever going to fit in?

Well, I was determined to fit in. In moving from country to country and settling down in this remote part of Canada, I experienced both pain and gain. The gains have made my life experience richer and more colourful than it otherwise would have been. The pain, however, was equally real and hurtful. I needed to figure out how to have the most gain with the least pain, and I did.

Recently, I was chatting on the phone with my friend Jay. Our friendship goes back to the mid-1960s, when we were both students at the Teacher Training University in Tehran. He went to the United States for a doctorate in TV production around the same time that I went to study for my MBA in Kansas. After he graduated, he went back to Iran to work as a producer on

Iranian National Television. A couple of years ago, he retired and moved to Vancouver, British Columbia. So he went from being Iranian to being a foreign student to being Iranian again, and then to being a newcomer in another country. While we were talking, he told me I should write a book about our experiences.

I have spoken to many people about this issue. Newcomers everywhere, not just those who move to a relatively small place, encounter novelty and discomfort. There are many experiences we share and problems we must overcome to succeed in our new home.

First, we need to adjust to a new place and a different culture. At the same time, we must get a job to make a living. While settling into our new home, we must learn to let go of some of the learned habits, values, and mindsets that do not work in our new environment, but we must do so without losing our real selves.

We must learn to be happy in ways we have not experienced before, through different community events, new sports, new connections, and new ways to spend our time. We must avoid avoidance. That is a signpost on the path to loneliness. What does that mean? We must not make excuses for why we cannot participate in our new culture. We must participate. Don't think you'll like the taste of the food? Eat it anyway. Miss walking through the jungle? Learn how to ski down a mountain.

We need to become fluent in the new language if we have moved somewhere where people speak differently. Nothing is so isolating as not being able to communicate with the people around you. While we are busy assimilating, though, we need to make sure we keep some of our own traditions and tastes—those things that keep us connected to our roots. Things like the music, art, and important dates and celebrations from our first culture should not be forgotten or discarded when we embrace our second.

We must avoid developing negative views about our new home. It does not matter whether it is the culture, the weather, or even the way people drive: that is our life now. It is too easy to blame our own loneliness on the new place rather than trying to overcome it. We must expand our horizons and not shrink from life by repeatedly going back to "the old ways."

I lived in the United States and in Ontario before I moved to Newfoundland. I managed okay, but I did not feel at home in either of those places. When I moved to St. John's, I wanted to feel at home. I wanted Newfoundland to be my home in every way. I wanted to be comfortable in my surroundings.

The way I did it was to become an NBC—a Newfoundlander By Choice—and not spend the rest of my life as a Come From Away. This was something I was committed to in my mind and in my attitude. How other people saw me did not matter. They could think of me as a CFA, but I refused to consider myself a stranger for the rest of my life, a guest in the place I had chosen as my home. I wanted, figuratively speaking, to be able to loosen my belt, put my feet up on the coffee table, and flick through all the channels on the TV—something guests would never allow themselves to do. So I set out to learn everything I could about being a Newfoundlander (as we call ourselves). I learned the culture, the customs, and the language (which is a unique form of English).

It took me about a year, but I did it. Yes, b'y, best kind! I connected with people, I volunteered on community boards, I attended every event possible. I gave free workshops and coached soccer. I did everything I could, including learning how to go mummering (an old Newfoundland Christmas tradition), and never turned down a chance to go out for fish and chips and beer with my colleagues.

I was careful not to pass judgment, even while I sensed I was being judged. If someone asked me where I was from, I answered "Cowan Heights," which is my neighbourhood in St. John's. If they pushed further, I told them I was from the west end. When they realized I was having fun with them, they would ask "Where was your home before?" I would tell them I came from the place of beautiful rugs and if they did not get that I would tell them I was from the place with beautiful cats. They usually got Persia after that, but I could go on and on until they figured it out or gave up.

At the same time as I was becoming a Newfoundlander, I retained some of my own traditions, such as Norouz, the Persian New Year, which falls on March 21. I give gifts on that day, as is the custom, and have gone into my children's schools to talk about Norouz and bring cookies, which is a Norouz tradition. (My children, as Newfoundlanders with a Persian father and Colombian mother, share in three cultures.)

These are things all newcomers can do to adjust to life in a new place. They are under our control. However, we also experience things that we have not brought upon ourselves—things we have no control over. These are the things that cause us a great deal of pain. We all cause pain for others, even if we do not mean to. Here are some of the pains that are inflicted upon newcomers, whether deliberately or unknowingly.

> **Discrimination based on colour, accent, name, dress, or behaviour**—This can manifest itself through passing judgment, blocking, giving the silent treatment, quietly ignoring someone, making them

wait longer, making sarcastic comments about them, asking them belittling questions, and using aggressive gestures and words.

Ignorance—This is manifested by not knowing, or knowing very little, about the newcomer and not bothering to learn. It entails not including them in events, not inviting them to participate, seeing them as different—"the other"—and stereotyping them. One way of harming someone through ignorance is not even bothering to learn how to pronounce their name correctly.

Attitude—Seeing oneself as superior and believing the newcomers are here to take away jobs and make the community unsafe. This can be seen in over-reacting to minor rule violations, over-correcting, and generally being closed-minded.

It is important to note that newcomers themselves are not immune to this behaviour. They may do the same to another immigrant or believe the same nonsense about another group. We must watch out for this. Having insight into our own attitude and behaviour is the key to adapting successfully.

Because I learned to become a Newfoundlander and a Canadian, I am twice as strong. I have my Persian heritage and I am also a Newfoundlander By Choice. I rejoice in both my identities. So when I go hiking (and Newfoundland is a beautiful place for hiking), I bring along packages of Persian dates to share with my buddies after dinner.

When we are on the trail and run into a stranger who asks where I am from, I hardly get the opportunity to answer before my buddies all shout out "Cowan Heights!"

11

Jackasses,
Brain Farts,
and a Magic
Srewdriver

BEING AN OCCASIONAL JACKASS

O N THE FARM in Aveh where I spent many months every summer when I was growing up, we had a lot of domestic animals. We had cows, sheep, horses, and we also had some jackasses, whose job it was to carry small loads around. Jackasses are not the most complicated animals. In fact, they are rather simple. Maybe that is why they are sometimes referred to as "stupid donkeys."

One thing you might not know is that jackasses can be quite noisy. I used to hear them singing in the fields and orchards— at least I called the sounds they made "singing," although not everyone might agree. I would listen carefully to their voices, and eventually I learned to "talk" to them by mimicking their singing, and they would answer.

I have no idea what we said to each other, but getting a donkey to sing is something I can still do. (I have since discovered that I can also talk to zebras in the same way. I do not know if the language they use is the same as that of jackasses, but they happily respond to my singing.) It is a bit of unexpected fun that I have entertained people with from time to time.

I do not know if jackasses are stupid—remember, I do not know what we are saying to each other—but they have that reputation. It is that reputation I am talking about when I say that I think most of us have a bit of jackass in us somewhere, which occasionally makes us do something stupid, turn our brain off, and not think through what we are doing.

A few years ago, I went into a pizza place after a long day of hiking with some friends. There was a beautiful young woman smiling from behind the counter and I asked her if I could have a large pizza. "Oh, no," she said. "You cannot have a large pizza. We close in thirty minutes, and it takes thirty-five minutes to make one."

I was a little puzzled by this, but I let it go. "Okay," I said. "Give me those five pieces of pizza from the rack of slices that have already been cooked."

"I'll have to charge you by the piece," she warned.

I was puzzled again. Why did she need to warn me of this? But I told her that was okay.

It turned out it was not so okay after all. The jackass she had inside her made her charge me five times instead of putting all five pieces on one bill. So I stood there while she rang in the first piece and then I swiped my card, put in my password, and waited for the transaction to go through. Then I did the same thing again. And again. And again. Five separate times.

I came out of that pizza joint pulling my hair—or at least I would have been pulling my hair if my hands were not full of pizza. But it was funny just the same. She was being such a jackass.

Another funny thing happened when I was walking the Camino Trail in Spain. Sometimes on the trail you are all alone, and sometimes you meet up with a person or a group of people and walk together for a while. I happened to be walking with a group of about ten people one day and had been chatting with a sweet and lively middle-aged woman. We walked about twenty kilometres together talking about our lives and our families. It was lovely. At one point, we came upon a farmer's field with about twenty cows and one lone jackass who, I learned later, was there to keep the cows calm. My own inner jackass suddenly emerged, and I said to my companion of the day, "Do you want me to talk to this jackass?"

She looked at me, surprised, and said, "Can you?"

"Yes," I told her. "Get your camera ready."

She got out her camera and called the other walkers over to witness me making an ass of myself. My inner jackass called out to the real jackass, who was very big, and he came over singing loudly and looking at me. The group was incredulous, surprised and amused. They took plenty of pictures as the two jackasses sang to each other, presumably in Spanish, at least on his part.

That night we all ended up staying at the same pilgrim hostel, and we sat together at dinner (the pilgrim's dinner was three courses with wine for about ten euros). The woman I had been walking with brought up my conversation with the jackass and how much fun it had been.

"You know," I said, "we all have a jackass inside us."

Across the table from me sat a big, pleasant fellow from Down Under who had not seen my earlier performance.

"Not me!" he cried. "I do not have any jackass inside me."

His girlfriend, who was sitting beside him, turned to him with a big smile on her face and said, "You have the biggest jackass of us all inside."

We all had a good laugh as our inner jackasses came out.

We must acknowledge the jackass we all have on the inside. It is a good thing, the fun side of your personality. Having fun with it is okay.

However, we must not let it run our lives the way some people do. Even real jackasses cannot sing all the time.

"SCREW" THIS!

ONE OF THE things I like to do in my practice is encourage people to have some kind of life picture. It is an internal and private picture that you can develop and see yourself in. You can add things to it and take things away as your desires and needs change and progress. So although some things may stay the same in this picture, others disappear. I think this is probably where the idea of the bucket list came from.

In some people's picture, they see themselves in a big house with many rooms. They have a fancy car (or maybe a few fancy cars), a boat, a skidoo, and all the other material things they value.

Others see themselves at the centre of a fancy wedding in a beautiful white gown or being the focus of a big birthday bash or other celebration.

Some imagine themselves as a great leader or a famous movie star or a championship hockey player.

A few see themselves working towards curing cancer or saving the environment or achieving world peace.

We all have secret ambitions and dreams. We may know we are dreaming with some of our desires, but it is still a good thing to have them, even if they are unattainable.

I have a secret dream. For the last fifty years I have dreamed of using a "screwdriver" on my patients. Something that, with a twist of the wrist, would turn depression into happiness, anxiety to tranquility, ignorance to wisdom, dysfunction to function, and disorder to order.

I have been looking for such a tool for ages. I have studied the various schools of psychotherapy, most of the psychiatric interventions available, and all the strategies I could find, because I do not want to miss out on anything that might help a patient of mine.

I know about the most controversial treatment, which is electroconvulsive therapy, or ECT, a brain stimulation technique that used to be called electroshock therapy. It is not like the old days. It has been refined so that it can work very well to treat many problems.

I know about transcranial magnetic stimulation, or TMS. In TMS, a device held above the head creates a magnetic field that causes a weak electrical signal to be applied to the prefrontal cortex, the region of the brain connected to mood. It works too.

Then there is vagus nerve stimulation (VNS), a treatment for depression that uses a surgical implant like a pacemaker to electrically stimulate a nerve, the vagus, that reaches up into the brain. It is used for treating epilepsy but may also be effective to treat depression.

As I said, I do a lot of research, so I know that there are many, many forms of therapy. Most of them started as a wish or secret dream of a doctor or researcher or therapist who wanted to do more to help patients.

In addition to knowing the limitations of my field of practice, I also know exactly what my own limitations are. I send patients to psychiatrists, to addiction counsellors, to other psychologists, even to personal trainers. I use any tool possible to help.

Occasionally a person comes to see me for one hour and that one hour is enough. They do not need to see me again. For example, one time a fifty-year-old man came to see me complaining of an attention problem. We went through all the tests, and he did seem to have mild ADHD—attention-deficit / hyperactivity disorder—so I told him to go to his physician and get some medication, but only as much as he needed to correct the problem. That was it. One hour was enough.

It does not always work out that easily. Sometimes I really, really want that screwdriver.

A few years ago, I had a middle-aged patient who had just about everything you could imagine would make for a happy life. But he'd had a dysfunctional upbringing and could not get over it. He suffered from a form of self-imposed self-hatred that left him isolated and depressed. He was convinced he was no good. He thought that if he was good, his father would not have mistreated him.

All my attempts at interventions and consultations had little effect. I could get him from point A to point B or maybe even to C, but no further. He still needed more. When I was with him, I often wished I had that magic screwdriver. I could put it in his ear and turn him into a happy-go-lucky man.

A lot of people in the world have their own screwdrivers. Some have a black one that turns them towards drugs, alcohol, gambling, and other self-destructive behaviours. Others have what I imagine to be green screwdrivers. These are the people who eat well, get plenty of exercise, and respond well to counselling. I have mentioned my screwdriver dreams occasionally, and some of my patients who have improved tell me the psychological screwdriver that I gave them really helped.

I am still looking for my fast golden screwdriver. I know I have done a lot of good over the years and solved a lot of issues. Nonetheless, I still wish I could do more. A small turn to the right. A little fiddling. Done. All better. Now go home and be happy. What a joy that would be.

YOUR DIRTY MIND

WHEN SOMEONE SAYS, "You've got a dirty mind," most people think the meaning is sexual. We think that a dirty mind belongs to a person who interprets everything in a sexual way or is always thinking about their desire or about forbidden sexual acts. This interpretation lends itself to the term "dirty old man." We do not think he will be good as new if he has a proper scrub in a hot bath—although maybe a cold shower would help!

But this is not what I mean when I say most of us have dirty minds. It has nothing to do with sex (in fact, it can interfere with sexual pleasure). The "dirt" in our minds is our negative feelings, and one of the biggest, dirtiest, most negative feelings we have is worry. Society accepts worry as normal. We worry about paying the rent, we worry about passing our exams, we worry about our health and our kids—boy, do we worry about our kids! You name it, we can worry about it, and we think there is nothing wrong with that. If we tell a friend we are worried, they confirm it is perfectly reasonable.

Worrying, for some people, is a way of staying on task. As if by focussing our attention on worrying, we are doing something about the problem. We somehow think that if we do not worry about an upcoming exam, we will not pass it. If we do not worry about our kids being out late at night, they will get into a car accident. However, this is not true. Worrying is just a bad habit. It does not solve anything. It's just playing in the dirt.

We can keep on worrying or we can clean up our minds. Worrying will not magically produce money to pay the rent. It will not give you the knowledge to pass your exams, and it certainly will not keep you healthy or your children safe.

I once had a patient who made such a habit of worrying about her children that it became one of her hobbies—right up there with cooking! She was a retired professional woman, and her four children were all fine: professionals themselves, married, and with children of their own. It did not seem as if there was any reason to worry about them. Nonetheless, she worried they would lose their spouses or lose their jobs or be bad parents. She did not worry about them physically, but she worried constantly about them messing up their lives. Somehow, she had come to believe that worrying was a charm against harm.

In the end, the choice was hers. She learned to manage her thinking. She made the decision to think about her children in a more positive light. Instead of imagining them being in an accident or hurt, she changed her thought pattern to think that they were just out and having fun.

Worrying is not a charm against harm. It is a dirty habit, and it does not lead to a solution. Worrying turns into rumination, which has no end and is just a coping mechanism. What does lead to a solution? Problem solving.

A few years ago, I was visiting my son, who lives in the United States. I went to stay with a cousin who lives nearby and his family for a few days. While I was there, I started peeing bright red urine. Naturally, I was worried. However, instead of just rolling around in the dirt of my mind, I searched for a solution. I asked my son to make me an appointment with a urologist so I could find out what was wrong. While I was waiting, I thought about what might have caused this sudden problem. My cousin and his family eat traditional foods that include a lot of beets. I realized that was the problem. I was not peeing blood—I was peeing beet juice!

As soon as I stopped eating so many beets, my condition miraculously cleared up. A visit to the urologist was no longer necessary. Instead of just worrying, I had come up with a practical way to confront the situation.

If something has you worried, sit down and try to come up with a solution to the problem. If you are worried about a long drive, check your tires and the weather forecast. If you are worried about your child going out at night, give them emergency funds. Find some way to address the problem rather than just worrying about it.

Of course there are many problems that are simply not in your scope to solve. Since you cannot do anything about them, it makes little sense to put energy into worrying over them. But breaking a bad habit is hard. People will worry even when there is no need. The patient whose hobby was worrying about her children could not just stop cold turkey. So we decided that once a day, she could spend one hour on worry. It was her misery time. If something worrying came to mind at any other time, she would say, "I'll come back at four p.m."

Sometimes, however, even that did not work. So I encouraged her to write down her really big worries and put them in an envelope—one worry per envelope. That gave the worry a physical form and a safe place to reside until we could talk about it. Often, by the time we got to a particular worry, it was not important anymore. It was just one more piece of dirt that had been swept away.

Sometimes it helps to see if worrying is justified by transferring it to someone else. I asked my patient what happened if her son was late coming home from work. She told me she would immediately start worrying that he had been in a car accident. However, when she applied the same situation to her son-in-law, she did not worry at all. She believed he must be sitting in a bar somewhere! When the subject was not the target of her worry (her own child), it was easy to imagine another scenario. Worrying about her son was just playing in the dirt. The less we allow ourselves to play in the dirt—or dwell in worry—the cleaner our mind becomes.

EMOTIONAL FAT

PICTURE A HIGH-RISE apartment building on a suburban street. It is the middle of the night and all is quiet, but things are not as peaceful as they first appear. In one apartment a young man, whose girlfriend left him two years ago, is lying in bed wide awake still thinking about her. In another, a young woman is tossing and turning because she cannot stop worrying about the job she was unjustly fired from six months ago. For another person, the reason for sleeplessness is a fight she had with her mother just before she died and the cruel thing she said to her. For someone else, the concern is a course at university that he did not pass.

For all of them, it is a real burden on their shoulders, something that happened that they cannot get over, that gnaws at them and that they continue to chew over. There is nothing they can do to rectify things. It is all in the past, but they cannot let it go.

I think of it as "emotional fat," something that needs to be burned or shed, just like physical fat. Because all it does is weigh you down.

I once had a patient who was not only professionally success-ful but happily married and a great father. But the emotional fat he carried around weighed him down and made his life miserable. When he was growing up, his father treated him very badly. The father treated all his kids badly—he probably carried a great deal of emotional fat around with him, too—but he treated this son particularly badly because he was the oldest. The son's mother was emotionally unavailable and did not seem to care.

Nonetheless, this patient continued to hope that one day he and his father could come to an understanding and have the kind of close relationship he thought fathers and sons should enjoy. Then the father got sick, and it looked like the illness was terminal. My patient sat by his father's bedside night after night so he would be there if his father needed anything. He sat there with his hopes and his dreams at the end of his father's life.

One night, at three o'clock in the morning, the father cried out, "Bobby! Bobby! Bobby!" My patient believed that this was it. That on his deathbed, his father would apologize for the way he had always treated his son and the two of them would be able to reconcile before it was too late. Hope swelled in his heart. Instead, when he responded, his father continued in the same old tone of voice that my patient had come to hate, "Get me a glass of water."

"It was the worst memory I had," he told me. Even though he was a great dad himself and had overcome the negativity of his upbringing, every time his father's name came up in conver-sation, he relived the anguish he felt at that moment when his father disappointed him for the very last time. He came to me to help him and the way I did that was by helping him to let the memory go.

Letting go is not the same as resolving. There is no solution to this problem. The man's father was dead, and they would never reconcile. That terrible disappointment, when his father lay dying, had happened, but it was in the past. There was never going to be another chance or a different outcome.

Trying to minimize, justify, or intellectualize an awful experience will not help. Coming up with a reason for why something happened does not work because it does not stop it from continuing to hurt. If the problem could be resolved, it would already have been, in those hours, days, and years spent chewing over it.

Sometimes getting rid of emotional fat is as easy as flushing a toilet. You can write down what is bothering you on a piece of paper, rip it into pieces, drop it in the water, and watch it circle the bowl once or twice before disappearing. You can achieve the same result by burning it and watching it turn to ashes. Do this repeatedly—as many times it takes. The important thing to remember is that you are getting rid of it—not solving it. You are making the memory lean, not letting the fat weigh you down. However, you need to recognize that it is fat in the first place and that you are in control—that you can say "enough is enough." You must give yourself permission to stop letting it hurt you.

Letting go does not mean forgetting. It means not letting it affect you in the present.

I had another patient whose son died at the age of thirty-five. By his vigilant care, this man had kept his son alive much longer than expected. Nonetheless, when his son died, the man tortured himself by constantly wondering what else he could have done and worrying that he had not done enough. He needed to let it go. And he needed to understand that letting go of the guilt and the anguish was not the same as letting go of his son. He was just letting go of the damage.

People do it all the time. Samuel Johnson was reported to have said that a second marriage is "the triumph of hope over experience," and he is right. People go through terrible divorces and then go on to remarry. They can do so not because they have forgotten their earlier experience of marriage, but because they have been able to let go of the suffering it caused them. Getting rid of the fat so they can fit nicely into their new wedding clothes.

BRAIN FARTS

MOST PEOPLE HAVE some idea about, or have seen people with, obsessive-compulsive disorder. It can take the form of repeatedly checking something, cleaning to excess every day, constantly organizing, and so on. Perhaps you remember the 1991 movie *What about Bob?* Bill Murray played Bob, who drove his psychiatrist, played by Richard Dreyfuss, bananas. It was a funny film, but in real life people with OCD are victims of the condition and are suffering. That is not funny.

I have seen my fair share of patients with full-blown chronic OCD problems, but I do not want to talk about those cases here. Rather, I wish to discuss those people with an egodystonic disorder. *Egodystonic* refers to thoughts and behaviours that conflict with the needs and goals of the ego or with a person's ideal self-image. It describes thoughts, impulses, and behaviours that are felt to be repugnant, distressing, unacceptable, or inconsistent with our own concept of ourselves.

I call them "brain farts."

Many years ago, I saw a retired man in his sixties. He was a respected person who had done well in life and raised his children with his wife, who was also his best friend. He had three grandchildren he loved dearly.

Then one day the thought came to him that he might sexually molest his grandchildren. He could picture it clearly. He was both scared and shocked by these thoughts. He tried to push them away, but the obsession that he would be unable to stop himself from abusing them grew. He decided to avoid his grandchildren completely so this horrible, unknown part of him would not get the opportunity to carry out the deed. When he finally came to see me, he had not seen the kids he loved so much for eight months.

I understood how much he loved his grandchildren and why he was avoiding them. OCD is the disease of doubt, and he needed to be certain he would not harm them.

I tried to explain what was going on in his brain.

Many of our body parts have their own actions. Our stomach growls, our skin sweats, and our nose sneezes. These are all involuntary. Our brain is the same. It can bring up irrelevant thoughts resulting from a mixture of neurobiological, genetic, and environmental conditions. These thoughts are ego alien, which means that they go against our own best interests and have nothing to do with who we are. They are only thoughts—a bunch of words and images that your brain put together.

I told my patient, "Your brain farted, and you gave it legitimacy. A fart is just a fart and has nothing to do with your possible future behaviour."

The problem was not so much that the thought had occurred

to him. It was that he had allowed it to become credible in his mind. Despite knowing better, he began to believe that he really could and would do this awful thing. That is where he went wrong. With a bit more explanation, he accepted this view and I watched the relief and happiness spread across his face. In later sessions, he told me that he had resumed seeing his grandchildren and was very happy.

We do not know with any degree of accuracy where these brain farts come from, but it seems some people have more of them than others. I have seen all sorts of these obsessions. Some are health-related, some are fear of doing harm or violence, some focus on safety and mortality. Health, sexuality, and safety are our three big concerns. We do not want anything to touch them, and we can develop phobias to protect them. It is also common for people with these kinds of problems to obsess about exactness, and when combined with an obsession about something else, like health, these thoughts can cause a real headache. For example, if you have one symptom that could indicate cancer, do you immediately assume that you do have cancer? If the thought pops into your head, and you accept it as valid, that is a brain fart.

I remember seeing a medical file (with permission, of course) that was at least three thousand pages long. The patient was a forty-five-year-old woman with no major health issues. Nonetheless, she visited the doctor constantly and presented with every imaginable disease or disorder. When I met her, she was a healthy woman who had no clue about obsessional thinking. She just lived her life searching for exactitude and certainty. Every time the smallest thought about a possible health concern entered her mind, she had to know if she was okay.

Real life, however, is uncertain. Nothing is exact. What a difficult life that meant for her. Fortunately, she had a calm and loving husband who had very few brain farts. Unfortunately, they had a teenaged son who was growing up to be more like his mother than his father in this regard. He had social anxiety and wanted to be sure what people thought of him before spending time with them. Because this was an impossible demand, he spent his time avoiding people.

In the end, the woman and her son learned to decrease the frequency and severity of their obsessional thinking. The mother did this through cognitive behaviour therapy, as she did not want to take medication. Her son, fortunately, because of his young age, willingness to change, and his mother's psychological insight, gained better control over his thoughts.

The solution to dealing with brain farts, as with so many other problems, is education and counselling to help differentiate between smart and creative thoughts and brain farts. Most people do not want their minds cluttered up with these thoughts. They need to know that they are not the only ones who have these terrible ideas invading their brains, and they need to learn how to avoid them.

Your brain is part of your body and can, in many ways, be treated the same way. If you fart a lot when you eat beans, then you learn to avoid beans. With counselling, our brains can benefit from a similar diet. Then if an occasional unpleasant or discomfiting thought pops up, we can dismiss it as the result of too many beans!

INBURSTS

HAVE YOU EVER watched a baseball game where the pitcher becomes irate and gets in the umpire's face—yelling, fit to be tied, looking like the worst thing in the world has just happened and the ump is personally responsible? Maybe you have seen a hockey player drop his gloves and go after a member of the other team, ready to beat him to a pulp?

In a way, these outbursts are all part of the show. The players know the camera and the fans are watching them. We've probably all experienced the same kind of thing, albeit to a much less dramatic degree. Our tempers flare and we have an outburst—and say something we shouldn't.

When that happens, it's a clear indication that something is wrong. After all, people do not just start yelling for no reason at all. Even if the reason is not a particularly good or valid one, an outburst gives cues about that person's state of mind for the people around them. In that sense, an outburst is easy. We can see it, so we can deal with it.

But what about the opposite? What about when someone represses their anger instead of letting it out? I call these inbursts, and they are more common than we imagine. In fact, I think they are more common than outbursts.

People with inbursts keep everything bottled up inside. Their emotions can run the gamut from annoyance, frustration, and indignation to infuriation, hostility, and rage. However, they often start with hurt, which leads to anger.

Hurt comes from missed expectations. I expect you to do something and you do not do it. Think of a scene where the one spouse hurts the other's feelings by forgetting their anniversary, for example. The spouse who has remembered the anniversary starts off hurt and quickly becomes angry. On the other side of the coin, hurt can come from someone doing something you do not expect them to do. Imagine being called into the boss's office expecting to be told what a good job you are doing and instead getting fired. Again, you begin with hurt and quickly move to anger.

Guilt is a similar emotion. It stems from doing, or not doing, something we think we should, or should not, have done. The spouse in the paragraph above might feel guilty about forgetting the anniversary. The boss might feel guilty about letting the employee go when he knows how much that person needed the job. One feels guilty for something he did not do and the other feels guilty for something he did do. In both cases that feeling can turn to anger, which can easily turn inwards, masking the pain of the guilt-ridden person. But, of course, such a build-up of inbursts will inevitably give off signals. People who experience inbursts may not start yelling at people, throwing down their hockey sticks and raising their fists, but they might get quite testy and touchy, act in a grumpy manner, and become moody. As well, their sense of mental balance can become skewed. They overestimate or underestimate a situation, either making mountains out of mole-hills or missing problems they should be paying attention to. They start to see everything in black and white; they overgeneralize. Everything can start to seem like a catastrophe waiting to happen, and they can become demanding and controlling.

It is quite common for depression to set in because the person with inbursts becomes angry with the world.

Sometimes, I must teach people how to let their emotions out—to replace inbursts with outbursts. I once treated a thirty-five-year-old woman with terminal cancer. People close to her were always trying to calm her down, but that was not what she needed. She needed the opposite. So I would take her out into the woods every couple of days, where we would be all alone. There, I encouraged her to vent and scream and hit things with sticks—to let it all out. She would pound on trees as hard as she could. It was exactly what she needed to deal with her anger, and it would allow her to remain relatively calm until the next session.

On occasion, I must help people recognize the emotions they have inside. I once treated a man who ran a highly successful business with his wife. Outwardly, he was immensely proud of them both—the business and his marriage. At least that is what he would say. However, it turned out that underneath that smiling and polite persona, he hated everything about his life. He had a mountain of anger built up inside him. I provided him with the tools, but it took a long time for him to realize that he wanted out—that inside the established businessman was a nomadic backpacker. When he finally walked away from his career, it made both him and his wife a lot happier.

The problem, at least from my perspective, is that people with inbursts are much less likely to seek the help of a professional like me, and that means I cannot help them.

How can people deal with their inbursts? Think of a tap. We need to keep our emotions warm. If they get too hot, we add a little cold water. If they get too cold, we add a little hot water. Some people need to get their emotions out physically, like my cancer patient, but most of us can gain the balance we need intellectually. Personally, I acknowledge the emotion; then, depending on the intensity of the feeling, I move myself to a safe place (this is often the washroom!).

It sounds simple, but talkers should talk, writers should write, and doers should do. Some people need someone to listen to them, a trusted person with whom they can pour out all their woes. Others can pour everything onto the page, journalling about their journey. Still others need a more physical approach, such as playing a sport or punching a pillow.

Interestingly, I have spoken to several soldiers who were drawn to that career because of some sort of childhood trauma. The military gave them the outlet they needed. As one said to me, "When I hit the target and hear the blast, I feel good." They have found an outlet for their inbursts.

The important part is recognizing what is going on. Then we can deal with it—or we find someone to help.

In the past couple of years, I have noticed I am growing a little more irritable. When I searched within myself, I discovered that my tolerance for bullshit is diminishing. I couldn't stop the bullshit, so I started looking for ways to help myself stay calm. I researched holistic medicines and techniques, learning about everything from kava root to lemon balm. Now I drink chamomile tea to help me relax.

Of course, even chamomile tea cannot cure everything. One awful afternoon, three couples in a row came to me seeking help to deal with the loss of a teenaged child. One o'clock. Two o'clock. Three o'clock. Two of the kids had died in accidents, and one from cancer. Each of these parents was experiencing overwhelming grief at the loss of their only child.

Over the course of those three hours, the intensity of the hurt I felt for these parents built and built until I began to rage inside.

After the third couple left, I could not see another patient right away. I told my administrative assistant to postpone my remaining appointments for half an hour. I went into my office, crying and angry, and closed the door behind me. Then I raised my fist into the air and started yelling at God for being so cruel, for allowing such tragedy to happen to people. I cursed and I swore, and I questioned everything about life. I did not expect an answer, but I got one anyway. "Get back to work."

What could I do? I went back to work.

Anger does not visit us for free. Even without counting its effect on our relationships with others, we pay for it physically. It promotes hypertension, cardiovascular disease, and a host of other diseases, any of which could prove fatal. That is a high price to pay for something we can learn how to deal with. A price that no one should be asked to pay.

YOU DON'T KNOW JACK

A N ATTRACTIVE YOUNG woman who has taken pains with her appearance—she is wearing her favourite red dress and has had her hair cut in a new style—is introduced to someone at a party. Instead of taking the opportunity to make a new friend, she immediately hears a little voice in her head saying, "She's prettier than you are."

Across the room, a young man has noticed the woman entering the room and would like to meet her. However, despite the fact that he has plenty of friends and is quite comfortable socially, when he tries to think of something to say to her, he hears a little voice warning him, "You are going to make a fool of yourself."

There was nothing wrong with the way the young woman looked. Similarly, there was no reason to believe that the young man would make a fool of himself. His friends could all attest to what a good conversationalist he was. Both people took something positive, which was their self-confidence, and turned it into something negative.

That is not unusual. Most of us are familiar with this kind of automatic negative self-conversation, even if we have never heard the term before. I have certainly been a victim.

When I was in high school, I was taught English, but I did not really learn it properly. In my twenties, before I moved to the United States to go to university, I hardly spoke the language at all. I really learned how to speak English then, but I will always have an accent, which used to be a real problem for me. Whenever I opened my mouth to speak among people for whom English is a primary language, I would hear that little voice in my head saying, "No one understands you" or "You are embarrassing yourself!"

I learned to call this little voice "Jack." It just seemed to fit. Some people call it Charlie. Some call it bastard. You can call it whatever you wish, but Jack suits me.

Many years ago, the vice-president of a large company consulted with me. He was a middle child who had been bullied in junior high school and whose father had not been emotionally warm (he probably had his own Jack to deal with). However, despite his less-than-ideal past, this man was an insightful, loving person. He once had a bit of social anxiety but had overcome it. Now he was consulting me because he was becoming increasingly anxious over performing important tasks in front of other people. He was especially anxious about giving presentations that impacted the lives of others, and the bigger the task, the more anxious he got. It was clear that Jack was whispering in his ear.

After a few sessions, when I understood his problem a little better, I jokingly told him, "Catch the bastard in action, and the next time he starts whispering in your ear, show him your middle finger!"

At first, he laughed at the idea of giving Jack the finger but doing this was a way to catch Jack in action and stop him in his tracks. He agreed to give it a try and it worked quite well. Using this technique, he became quite good at thwarting Jack.

Jack might never completely go away, but he can be overcome. Everyone has their own inner "Jack." This critic has been validated throughout our lives by critical teachers, parents, and society. This inner critic starts to sound like a normal voice, but it excels at undermining your self-confidence. There are three Cs that can help you overcome the little voice in your head: catch it, confront it, and change it.

The hardest part is catching Jack in action, since most people do not even recognize they are doing it—remember, it is self-criticism: we are doing it to ourselves. So how do we recognize that Jack is approaching? If you feel nervous, Jack is preparing to strike. If you are hurt, angry, or fearful, Jack is by your side, ready to start whispering those terrible things in your ear. Jack accompanies negative feelings.

Once you have caught Jack, the next step is to confront him. This is where giving Jack the finger comes in. Stop him in his tracks and do not allow yourself to become anxious. Confront your embarrassment, your anger, your insecurity, and do not let it take over. The more you persist in your endeavour to change the voice from negative to positive, the less anxious you will feel.

Finally, change the voice in your head. Some of my patients even use my voice to keep Jack from gaining the upper hand! By doing so, you change yourself. You are not letting negative emotion rule your actions.

My advice to the successful vice-president had unforeseen consequences, and thinking about it still makes me laugh. A few weeks after he started giving Jack the finger, he came into my office for his appointment with a big grin on his face. I knew he had had a particularly important meeting that week and I was curious to know what was up.

"I was driving along that morning on one of the main streets and Jack started attacking," he told me. "I was talking back and showing my middle finger while I was driving. This went on for five minutes. When I stopped at a red light suddenly, I saw the woman driving next to me showing me middle finger and muttering the F-word. It was obvious what she thought, and I could not stop laughing, which made it worse."

I could not help myself, and I laughed along with him. Sometimes it is funny how others perceive our actions.

This technique proved remarkably successful for the businessman, and it gave him the upper hand in defeating that little voice. Fortunately, he eventually learned to give Jack the middle finger mentally instead of physically. I wonder if the woman in the car ever tells people about the man she once drove beside who was very rude to her for no reason at all.

I hope this experience hasn't fuelled her own inner "Jack."

THE BASEBALL BAT

ONE DAY, A very handsome man came to see me for advice. He was in his late forties, and he seemed to have a perfect family life, with a beautiful and kind wife and two teenaged kids whom he got along with. So, why did he need my help? Because his perfect family life was not good enough for him.

He had always been a philanderer and did not seem to think there was anything wrong with that. His father was the same way and so were his brothers. They bragged about it among themselves, and it was as if they had a little adultery club that their wives knew nothing about.

Throughout my patient's married life, he had affairs. None of them had been serious—at least as far as he was concerned. They ranged from one-night stands to relationships that lasted a few weeks. He was extremely charismatic, and I thought he must have earned a doctorate in picking up women.

However, his string of affairs was not the problem—at least not as far as he was concerned. At the age of forty-five, he met a twenty-seven-year-old woman and developed an intimate relationship with her that went beyond sex. Instead of breaking up before things had a chance to grow serious, he kept seeing her and even told her he would leave his wife. This went on for three years, and he could not bring himself to break things off with her. At the same time, he did not want to leave his wife and commit to a monogamous relationship with this new woman, which is what she would have insisted on. It was being trapped in this romantic triangle that had brought him to see me. He wanted me to somehow fix things for him, to make his problem go away.

I listened to his story, and after discussing issues of morality and ethics, I told him, "I see a man in front of me who stuck a very large baseball bat up his ass with his own hand. Now this man is asking me: 'Should I stick it farther in or pull it out?'" I told him that if he kept this up, soon that bat would be sticking out of his mouth.

He needed that graphic visual to see how much harm he was doing to himself.

We shove baseball bats up our own asses all the time, by which I mean we are experts at getting ourselves into trouble.

We add trouble to our lives that is completely unnecessary. Maybe, like this man, we have affairs and become trapped between our lovers and our spouses. Maybe we buy a house that is too big for our income and lie in bed worrying about how to pay the mortgage.

It's easier to avoid than you think. If you are the kind of person who wants to indulge in a series of one-night stands, then do not get married. If you want a big house, make sure you have the income for it or else buy something smaller. We need to accept responsibility for our actions and stop complicating our lives.

People make life hard for themselves by not realizing that they are the ones sticking the baseball bat up their own asses, and they are not the only ones who suffer; their families suffer too. Then they expect someone to come along and fix it for them.

I only saw the man with the baseball bat that one time, or at least I only saw him once professionally. A few months after our meeting, I ran into him at a shopping mall. He came up to me to tell me how he was doing. He had extricated himself from the long-lasting relationship and was now back to having short-term, no-strings-attached flings.

What he told me did not surprise me. I knew he would do that, and I did not follow up. I just politely walked away. I am not a morality doctor.

TO PEE OR NOT TO PEE

THE OTHER DAY, I went to see my urologist. I have been having little visits with him for fifteen years now. Sometimes I think I see him more often than I see some members of my own family, and considering what he does for a living and where he puts his enormous fingers, I know we have a more intimate relationship.

Going to the urologist is not very much fun, and I am not the only person who thinks so. A few years ago, I had an early-morning appointment, and when I arrived there were three other men sitting in the waiting room—all over six feet and all scowling. I sat down next to one of them and said, "Nice day." He glared at me. "You're kidding," he said.

"I'm scared, too," I replied.

He looked at me for a minute and then muttered, "Have you seen the size of his hand?!" I will never forget the look on his face.

The reason my urologist and I are on such close terms is that I have an overactive bladder. I pee about four times more often than the average man. (I wonder whose job it was to count how many times people typically go the washroom so that they could come up with this statistic.) When I am out in public, in a new restaurant or coffee shop, for example, the first thing I do is locate the door with that discreet little stick man on it, so I know exactly where to head when the inevitable urge comes upon me.

There is nothing wrong with me. I do not have cancer or anything—just a close, personal relationship with washrooms. But we all have one physical problem or quirk that becomes the centre of our attention; this is mine. A few years ago, while preparing to climb Mount Kilimanjaro, I kept hoping there would only be men in my expedition group so I would not be embarrassed in front of a woman. How is that for dwelling on a problem?

I have turned it into a joke. I call myself "Don Juashroom" and think of going to the washroom as taking a little break, having some "me" time.

So it is kind of funny that I once had a patient with the opposite problem. He was a man of twenty-five, single and soft-spoken. He had a gentle soul—and an inability to go to the washroom in public. It seems to be a problem only men have. I have never met a woman with this issue.

For this patient, it all started in high school (just like so much else). He would have to pee, and he would get teased. He started to believe that people were evaluating him, judging how much he peed or how he stood or something. Eventually, it got to the point where he was unable to pee in a public washroom at all.

This is a quite common problem.

People tell themselves that it is not them—it is the washroom. It is dirty or unhygienic—anything they can think of to shield themselves from having to accept that the problem is with them.

This young man was the same way, but his problem was really starting to impinge on his life. He worked in construction and only took on jobs where he could work alone or get back to his own home in a timely manner. Going out socializing became more and more difficult. It is hard to go clubbing when you can only stay out a little while before you must go home to use the toilet. Finally, he came to see me because that is no life for anyone, never mind a twenty-five-year-old.

The first thing he had to do was confront the belief that people were watching him. It was irrational, unless he really was doing something wrong or odd, which he was not. This was an exceedingly difficult thing for him to do. Then I got him to imagine he was using a public washroom. He kept imagining it over and over until he was able to actually go into one. It was not easy because he had been nurturing and building this phobia for ten years, but he finally managed it. I slowly helped him conquer peeing in a diversity of places, including outside and in mall washrooms. I even went out with him for a beer and then went to the washroom with him. But one threshold he could not cross was the one that led to the washroom in a restaurant.

To cross this highest of hurdles, I had him make a list of one hundred restaurants and told him he had to use the washroom in each one of them, and he had to go to at least three of them every single day.

"Once you get the first fifty or sixty over with, the rest will go very quickly," I assured him.

Now, after ten years of hiding, he is well on his way to being able to stay away from home long enough to work and have a social life.

As for the trip up Mount Kilimanjaro, there was a woman in my group after all. My heart fell when I saw her, and she somehow figured out why. She took me aside to tell me that I had nothing to worry about compared to her. She was walking around with a portable penis in her pack so she would not be embarrassed as the only woman in a group of men by having to squat. I guess we all need a bit of help sometimes when it comes to basic bodily functions.

RECIPE FOR RESILIENCE

OUR BODIES CAN be so embarrassing, and I do not mean the way they look. I mean the way they act—especially when we are out in public. Put your hand up if you ever accidentally passed gas in front of other people and then looked around casually as if searching for the culprit. Sometimes that very embarrassment can be applauded.

Have you ever been for a colonoscopy? If you have, you already know what I am talking about. The whole procedure starts out by stripping you of all your dignity—and things go downhill from there. During the procedure, a camera is inserted into your rectum and wriggled around, forcing air into your colon. Well, like they say, what goes up must come down. When the examination is finally over, and you think you cannot feel any more humiliated, they suddenly tell you to fart. Yes, fart. Right there in front of them! You cannot help yourself; you do it. And you know what? That is a good thing. It means you are bouncing back from the procedure. It means you are resilient. It means you are returning to normal.

But, just as physical resilience is important, we also need psychological resilience.

Resilience has been defined as "the process of, capacity for, or outcome of successful adaptation despite challenging or threatening circumstances."[3] In other words, resilience is the ability to adapt well to stress, adversity, trauma, or tragedy. It means that you remain stable in the face of disruption and turmoil and stay healthy on both a psychological and physiological level.

If you are resilient, you may go through temporary disruptions in your life, like not being able to sleep well, when faced with challenges, but you are still able to carry on with your daily tasks. You remain generally optimistic about life and rebound quickly.

I have asked several people what they believe resilience is and how we can achieve it. Some believe you are born with it. Others think it is something you can develop. Though science has not answered this question yet, I believe it is the latter. In this case,

[3] Masten, A., Best, K., & Garmezy, N. (1990). Resilience and development: Contributions from the study of children who overcome adversity. Development and Psychopathology, 2(4), 425-444.

nurture wins over nature.

Resilience can apply to all parts of our life: our physical health, our mental and psychological health, our relationships and families, our work health, our spiritual health, our relationship with nature and, of course, our financial health.

We need to be resilient to get over illness, to get over a failed relationship, to get over losing a job, and so on. We need resilience to recover from all the setbacks that inevitably occur in life.

Resilient people have certain characteristics:

- They can adapt to change easily and feel in control of their lives.
- They bounce back after hardship or an illness.
- They have close, dependable relationships.
- They remain optimistic and do not give up, even if things seem hopeless.
- They can think clearly and logically under pressure.
- They can see the humour in situations, even stressful ones.
- They are self-confident and feel strong.
- They can handle uncertainty or unpleasant feelings.
- They know where to turn for help.
- They like challenges and feel comfortable taking the lead.

Obviously, all these characteristics are good things. To achieve them would make our lives so much better. The good news is that since resilience is part of how we are nurtured—not embedded in our nature—it can be learned. We can all become more resilient.

Resilience is like a muscle. To build it, we have to strengthen it, just as people do push-ups or lift weights. When we start to get good at these exercises, we increase the amount we lift or the number of repetitions we do. The result is that we end up stronger and we stay stronger. It is our struggle that gives us that strength.

I have lost a child, a sibling, parents, friends, co-workers, and patients. The grief and sadness I felt forced me to seek meaning in my life. The only alternative was hopelessness and despair. So I developed my resilience, and I am not the only one who has done so. I had a discussion with a patient of mine about this a little while ago. He was close to me in age and had been coming to see me for twenty-five years. These days, he comes mostly for a "tune-up" because, generally, he is coping fine with life. However, that had not always been the case. He went through a severe depression in his forties. He had five children and ended up losing both his job and a battle over his insurance coverage. It took him about five years to get past these setbacks, but in the end, he was more efficient, a better parent, more reasonable, and less entitled. In other words, he became a better person—a person he would not have been without these setbacks and without his struggle to develop resilience.

What are the push-ups and deep knee bends we must do to build resilience? What weights must we lift to keep ourselves bouncing back in the face of adversity—and to stop us from falling into a pit of despondency?

Over the years, I have developed a kind of recipe for resilience. These suggestions have proven effective for my patients, and the physical aspects have been found to be effective by medical doctors and scientific studies. My recipe is a composite of my professional and personal experience. Some of the ingredients are mental. Some are physical. All are worthwhile.

My "Recipe for Resilience"

- Take no less than a hundred and fifty minutes a week to get moving—walking, cycling, swimming, and so on.

- Eat a rainbow diet—lots of colours on your plate! I recommend including plenty of deep-water fish.

- Take general vitamins, fish oil, omega-3, and specific vitamins like D (especially in the winter) and B complex.

- Spend less time on the computer, in front of the television, or glued to a phone screen.

- Spend time in and with nature. Go for a walk in the woods or the park; garden, go for a swim, even take a bath to feel water on your skin.

- Seek out and nurture good and rich relationships with other people.

- Teach your brain to be happy by re-experiencing the small joys in life: a baby's smile, stirring music, a funny joke . . . Do this approximately every three hours for a few minutes.

- Learn different kinds of relaxation strategies. You can find many techniques described online—see what works for you.

- Take time for recreation, for play, for fun, to cultivate positive emotions.

- Seek out spirituality—this does not have to be a particular religion, although it can be; it is really about opening your mind to other possibilities and contemplating other realities.

All these practices will help to build resilience, and they will help to keep it strong.

As with any muscle, we must keep flexing our resilience or it will get flabby. Many years ago, I was having one of those bad days. It started off with an argument with my wife, a crying baby, and getting to work late. The day did not get any better, and by the time I headed for home I had had enough. I thought, *what else could go wrong?* Then, while crawling in traffic, I heard the wail of a police siren. I pulled over and cursed at the sky—"I wasn't challenging you to make my life even worse!" When the officer got to my car, I told him indignantly I had not done anything wrong. Oops. It seems I had turned right on a road that was clearly marked "no right turn on red."

I could not keep all my troubles and woes to myself any longer. I told him all about all the bad things that had happened to me that day, starting with getting up late and ending with him pulling me over. When I got to the end of my tale of woe, he looked at me carefully and then said, "Nice story. That is an eighteen-dollar fine."

What could I do? I could either continue in a downward spiral or pull myself up and laugh. I decided to flex my resilience muscle, bounce back, and laugh. I still laugh when I think about that day and that cop with his laconic reply to my outpouring of affliction. "Nice story."

CRANKING DOWN THE PAIN

WE HAVE ALL walked through a room in our home without paying too much attention to where we are going. It is a familiar place, and we feel safe there. Suddenly, we step on a Lego block that did not get tidied up with the rest, and a sharp corner jabs into the arch of our foot. Or maybe the coffee table has been pushed out of place, and our toe makes sudden contact with its very hard leg. Ouch! For just a second the pain is excruciating. We may curse, swear, exclaim, or hop about as we rub our injured foot, but then we move on. We get so wrapped up in what we are doing that we completely forget about how much we hurt only moments ago.

Another time, we wake up with a splitting headache. We frown, rub our temples, and either take some pain medication or try to ignore the pounding. A little while later, our spouse asks how we feel and we notice, perhaps with a bit of a pleasant surprise, that the headache has cleared up. We were distracted and forgot about the pain until it went away by itself.

Sometimes, however, pain does not go away by itself. Sometimes pain is something that a person must live with day in and day out. It can become their only reality.

An old advertisement spoke about "the heartbreak of psoriasis." What a strange phrase. Psoriasis is a skin condition. It has nothing to do with heartbreak. Yet the term is still in use (even if ironically), despite being coined over fifty years ago. Perhaps it struck a chord because physical ailments can have an extraordinarily strong mental and emotional effect.

Biologically speaking, pain is a signal that the body has been hurt. When the pain does not go away, we call it chronic pain. This occurs when the pain mechanism itself goes awry. This can be caused by certain conditions or diseases such as back or neck pain, diabetic neuropathy (damaged nerves due to diabetes), fibromyalgia, interstitial cystitis (bladder pain), as well as other chronic conditions.

Chronic pain can create a whole host of other physical symptoms like fatigue, heart problems, weight problems, insomnia, and aching. But it can also cause a lot, maybe more, mental health problems including depression, anxiety, feelings of hopelessness and helplessness, and low self-esteem. These can affect every part of our lives from our work to our hobbies, from our daily activities to our vacations, from our social lives to our sex lives.

It can be exceedingly difficult to change our lives and our habits in the face of chronic pain. When we can no longer participate in our regular activities, we can easily become isolated. We can lose friends if our only connection with them was through activity such as playing sports. When the activity is gone, so is the friendship. Other friends just do not have an interest in our illness and drift away.

We can also have difficulty accepting that we can no longer do what we used to take for granted. I had a patient who became very irritable because he was used to being a strong man in his forties and now he had to look for a bench every hundred feet when he was walking through the mall so he could rest. It was the change in his condition that he hated, and as a result he was constantly barking at his wife and daughter, who eventually both started barking back. However, his pain and incapacity were his new reality, and he had to face it.

So, what can we do about it?

In her book, *Managing Pain before It Manages You*, Dr. M. A. Caudill explains the mind and body connection: "Chronic pain certainly fits the definition of adverse chronic stress. The effects of chronic stress are felt to be the results of a prolonged fight-or-flight response."

She recommends using all the techniques of stress management, including relaxation responses such as positive phrases, positive imagination, relaxing through music, repetitive motion, and creating safe places by visualization. All these help to decrease feelings of pain.

In contrast, decreasing physical activity and socialization, along with increasing isolation and negative or self-defeating thoughts and feelings that result from chronic pain, can cause the feeling of pain to increase. Nobody wants that!

So how do I help my patients stop their pain from escalating? One of the things I say on a regular basis is "do not crank it up." Do not make the pain out to be bigger than it actually is.

A long time ago, a man came to see me and the first words out of his mouth were: "Doc, I could not sleep last night." When I asked him why, he told me it was because "the damned faucet was leaking!" This patient lived right next to the airport and had planes passing overhead all the time, even at night. As you can imagine, I was surprised to hear that a kitchen tap would keep him awake. He dismissed this argument, saying that the sound of the planes was a noise he was used to.

He was right, but to me that meant that he told his brain not to process the sound of planes passing overhead, so his brain got used to not hearing them. However, he did not tell his brain not to process the noise from the tap because it was new, and he was disturbed by it all night. He had learned how to crank down the sound of the planes, but he cranked up the sound of the faucet.

Pain patients always tell me how much it hurts, how very painful their body has become. The problem is that when they do this, they are not just telling me—they are telling themselves, too. Focusing too much attention on the pain can crank it up, so that a pain that began as a three out of ten soon climbs the scale. I explain this to my patients and help them learn to crank it down; many of them are quite successful in controlling their pain this way.

Society is not particularly good at teaching us to take pleasure in small things. But we should. I tell my patients the following: Teach your body pleasant feelings by re-experiencing the small pleasures repeatedly. Small things like seeing a baby smile, tasting good food, hearing a beautiful song, touching something soft and warm, and swimming in warm water are all pleasant. When a pleasant thing happens, go over it again and again in your mind several times a day. Your mind will become so busy concentrating on all the good feelings (instead of dwelling on all the negatives) that the pain will no longer be the central focus of your life.

This is extremely important. If we cannot fix our bodies, then we must fix our brains by changing the narrative—turn the negative into something positive. I used to live with chronic pain due to a stomach condition. I consoled myself by saying that at least it stopped me from drinking!

Hiking is one of my greatest pleasures. However, when I am climbing a hill with a forty-pound pack on my back, I can feel quite a bit of pain after several hours of travel. Instead of concentrating on the pain, I think about the scenery, the fresh air, and the joy I have being with my hiking buddies. This helps to overcome any pain I might be experiencing.

Last year when I was visiting my son and his family, I took my grandson Nico out for a walk. We had gone about two kilometres when Nico, who was three and a half at the time, decided he wanted to sit on my shoulders. I agreed, thinking it would be temporary. I was mistaken. It turned out he was done and expected me to carry him the rest of the way home. Now Nico is a well-built, sturdy boy and it was hard on my shoulders to carry him all that way. But at the same time, it was a good experience. I told myself that he was enjoying our time together and I was incredibly lucky to be able to carry him all that way at my age. It is a great memory for me, and I hope it is something Nico will remember fondly as well.

In making that memory with Nico, I took the focus away from the pain. Sufferers of chronic pain must learn to do this, too. They must accept their limitations and celebrate their capabilities—the things they are still able to enjoy. Perhaps some friendships have been lost, but the joy of music, for example, may have been found. Perhaps household chores must be reassigned, but it is a perfect opportunity to say goodbye to doing the laundry and hello to managing the finances. (Who knew numbers could be so fascinating?)

We cannot make the pain go away, but we can minimize its effect on our lives. There is always something positive to be found, if we look hard enough. When I see a patient, I see the whole person, not just their problem. I think of each person as a garden, and sometimes they need my help to get rid of the weeds. We all have beautiful flowers growing in us—we just need look in the right place.

A QUICK COURSE IN TREATING CAR ACCIDENT VICTIMS

D O YOU KNOW that awful split-second feeling when you are in a car, either as the driver or as a passenger, and it looks like an accident is inevitable? Maybe an animal has run out onto the road and you are frantically trying to stop or swerve. Maybe the person in the rear-view mirror does not seem to have realized that you have stopped for a light. Maybe the driver of the car in front of you has just slammed on their brakes and you are desperately trying to do the same while skidding sideways on a patch of ice. There are so many scenarios, and we can picture them very easily.

That is not surprising. As of 2017, there were 34.4 million cars registered in Canada. Those big hunks of metal and glass screaming down the roads in all directions accounted for 154,886 reported injuries in that year alone, and this number does not include the countless little fender benders that happen almost routinely and result at best in a shrug and at worst in the exchange of insurance documents.

When we hear there has been a car accident, the first thing we want to know is whether anyone was hurt and, if so, how seriously. When we wonder about this, we are usually thinking about physical injury. Though it does not always happen, people get hurt psychologically, too. It may not be a growing problem, but it is a problem that is gaining more prominence. In fact, as I was beginning to write this chapter, the local CBC morning show ran a piece about automobile insurance hikes and how they were becoming necessary because so many victims were claiming compensation for psychological injury.

In some cases, the severity or even the existence of such injuries is questioned. If a person is claiming psychological injury, the insurance company wants proof. The family physician, a psychiatrist, or a psychologist is called in to confirm the injury and its severity.

That is how I often get involved with these cases. I have taken part in the assessment and treatment of many post-accident patients, and I have come to believe that our mental and emotional health gets hurt when we are involved in an accident, whether the body is hurt or not.

Victims of an accident may feel a range of emotions:

- an inability to forget the impact, resulting in numbness
- distress
- fear
- worry
- an inability to relax
- mood swings
- irritability
- sadness or general upset
- anger of a passenger towards the driver or the driver of the other vehicle
- guilt
- shame
- self-blame or blaming others
- low concentration
- not wanting to talk, social withdrawal
- rumination
- flashbacks

These emotions can result in physical symptoms:

- insomnia
- nightmares
- racing heartbeat
- dry mouth
- low energy, tiredness
- body tension
- pain
- headaches
- upset stomach
- occasional crying
- hypervigilance

People may not experience all these symptoms, and in most cases the effect is transitory. However, for some people, these symptoms persist. I know some physicians who send their patients to me for screening, but I wish all of them would send their patients for psychological help if they are complaining of any of these issues. Many accident victims do not speak up until the symptoms become more pronounced.

I have several patients who, a year or two after a motor vehicle accident, are still not driving or are limiting their driving to certain places. They have frequent flashbacks, sleep problems, and high anxiety. Not only that, but these symptoms sometimes bring other bad memories and traumas back to the forefront, which destroys normal life. This complicates the necessary psychotherapy, especially when the patient's physical injuries cause chronic pain and continued dysfunction.

Usually, in cases like this, insurance companies, injury lawyers, other paralegal professionals, and health professionals are involved. The claim process, which includes a lot of paperwork, independent assessment, and review, ends up causing more severe stress for the person who is already suffering.

After seeing so many accident victims, I feel I have enough data to write an entire book on that experience alone. Of course, this has an impact on me as well. For example, there are times when I feel pressure from insurance companies and their rehabilitation agents campaigning for more and more information. They repeatedly want copies of my notes, copies of my test results, and letters giving my opinion. I feel my role changing from that of psychologist to paper pusher and information counter for all the other interested parties. But in my mind, I am there to help the patient get better, not serve as an agent of the insurance company. That can be very taxing.

I have a few things I do to get a handle on all this extra work-load. First, I stay informed about all the issues related to motor vehicle accidents—I listen, I read, and I search everywhere I can for information. I make sure I understand the boundaries of my professional ethics.

Not only am I clear about what my role is, I want to be certain that my patients understand what I can and cannot do. I also do the same with the other players: lawyers, insurance companies, rehabilitation agencies, and everyone else involved must be aware of my limitations. I cannot allow myself to crumble under their demands.

I have learned not to be pressured by time or the demands of others.

I have learned to be better at my job. Early in my career, I had a patient I never managed to persuade back into a vehicle after a nasty accident. Looking back, I think that if he came to see me now, I could probably help him overcome that fear.

Treating victims of car accidents is an eye-opening experience. I have become a much more careful driver as a result!

TO FEAR IS HUMAN

THERE IS ONE thing that everybody in the world has in common. It is not the belief that our mother is the best cook in the world (well, okay, maybe we all share two things in common!). What I am talking about is fear. We are all afraid. All of us.

There are so many things to be afraid of. We can be afraid of being harmed, of death, of being judged, and of failure. We can be afraid of just about anything.

Being afraid is not the same as being anxious. Most of my patients come to see me because they are anxious about something. They have performance anxiety, social anxiety, sexual anxiety, all kinds of anxieties. Others come because fear is stopping them from enjoying life.

I had a young man come to see me who was letting his fear of rejection run—and, therefore, ruin—his life. He was twenty-seven years old; he had four university degrees and a good job. In fact, he had everything but a girlfriend. He told himself he was too busy to date, but the truth is he was just afraid to ask a girl out. He was letting his fear make decisions for him and, by doing so, he was missing the opportunity to live a full life.

We cannot get away from being afraid. We live in fear and our fear is used against us all the time. Dictators know how to use fear. That is how they rule. But there are other, more subtle forms of fear that we live with every day. Our parents teach us fear even if they do not mean to. That is what a lot of religion is about. You will go to hell if you do (or don't do) this or if you behave in a certain way.

We learn not to steal at a young age, but how does that lesson become instilled? Consequences. We become afraid to steal.

Even something as simple as paying our bills is motivated by fear. We do not pay them on time just because that is when they are due. We pay them because if we do not, we will have to have to pay interest or have the service cut off. First our parents, then society teach us to be afraid. So it is not surprising that our fear can get out of hand.

Being afraid is a normal feeling for all creatures, and human beings are no exception. You can't just stop being afraid, because fear will never stop. That is just going in the wrong direction. Humans can use their intelligence to overcome their fear, and that is important. Because if we give in to our fears, we stop enjoying our life. Instead, we must do things even though we are afraid. A brave person is not someone who is not afraid. A brave person is someone who feels fear and carries on.[4]

As mentioned earlier, I have a life list, and one of the things on that long-running list was a trip to Antarctica. I wanted to visit the South Pole! In 2012, some friends and I decided to make the journey together. It was a big undertaking and we planned very carefully. Even getting to the tip of South America, from where our boat would take us on the last leg of our journey, involved a lot of travel—St. John's to Toronto, Toronto to New York, New York to Santiago, Santiago to Buenos Aires, and finally Buenos Aires to Ushuaia in Tierra del Fuego, Argentina, the southernmost city in the world. We finally boarded the ship to take us to Antarctica at five o'clock in the evening. We had come so far and now faced a two-day trip to reach our much-anticipated destination.

The Southern Ocean, which is also called the South Polar Ocean, can get quite rough. I had heard that on a roughness scale of one to ten, this ocean can be a ten. I doubt it was more than a five on the scale that night, but the ship was rocking, and not in a good way. I got up to use the bathroom (of course) and the ship's movement made me bang my leg on the door so badly it started bleeding. By midnight, in my small cabin with my friend snoring just feet away from me, I could not sleep. Fear grabbed hold of me.

---

[4] Psychologist Susan Jeffers wrote an extremely good book called *Feel the Fear and Do It Anyway* (Ballantine Books, 1987) about overcoming our fears.

I thought about how I was on a tiny ship in the middle of the ocean in one of the most isolated places in the world: "How could I be so stupid as to put myself in this dangerous position?" The fear grew and grew—greater than I have ever felt before. What was a possibility—that the ship might sink—became, in my mind, a probability. The ship would sink! I knew I had to do something to calm myself down, but I could not stop being afraid. Fear is something we live with all the time. So I put my intelligence to work to overcome it.

I said to myself, "This is a normal fear because I am doing something I have never done before. This ship makes this trip every week and the crew has been working on it for many years. They are not stupid people; they just do not validate their fear." Thus, I reasoned that if the people who were experts at making this journey, who knew so much more about it than I did, were able to do so calmly, then I could as well. I would leave myself in their capable hands. This put a stop to my fight with fear, and I was able to go to sleep. The next thing I knew, we were being called to breakfast. Perfectly safe.

Life is full of warnings. We hear so much more about the things we should not do than we hear about the things we can do. We need to stop validating this fear. To validate our fear is to let it win, and to let it win, to chicken out, is a one-way road to lost opportunities.

Fear is always there. We must choose for ourselves whether to let it rule our lives.

UNDERSTANDING OTHER WORLDS

A VISITOR TO a mental hospital parked his car in front of the building and when it was time to leave, he saw that he had a flat tire. There was a group of patients hanging around in front of the hospital talking and smoking and, for want of anything else to do, watching the man. They saw him take his spare tire out of the trunk, remove the flat, and replace it. But when the man went to screw the nuts back on to the new tire, they were not to be found anywhere. Perhaps there was a joker in the crew watching him who had taken them. In any case, the man stood there trying to figure out what to do. Finally, one of the patients, who had been watching, approached him and suggested, "Take one nut from each of the other wheels and use them to hold the tire until you can get to the store and buy more."

The man was impressed by this quick and clever solution and told the patient so: "How did you know to do that?" he asked.

"I am supposed to be crazy, not stupid," was the laconic reply.

Of course, this is just a story, but it is true in one way. People may have mental illnesses, but that does not mean they are not smart. When I was younger, I was fascinated by life in the mental hospital. I worked in mental hospitals for many years, and I learned a great deal from the patients, residents, and my co-workers, including the fact that intelligence has nothing to do with mental illness. They taught me more than I ever learned in school.

I eventually came to see that there are basically three types of mental illness. (I should mention that I am not talking about people with psychopathic personalities—those who are totally self-centred and believe "mine is mine and yours is mine, too, and I get to take it from you by whatever means I chose." These people lack both empathy and respect for anyone, and I did not include them in my grouping here.)

I divide those with mental illness into three rough groups:

1. People who live in the real world but have mental health issues. They may have high or low moods and all kinds of fears and problems with their behaviour, but they are rooted in reality.

2. People who live in a different world. These are people like those with schizophrenia, who hear and see things that do not exist in the real world.

3. The people in between. They suffer from problems such as borderline personality disorders. They sometimes go back and forth between the real world and their own.

Notice that I say these are people with problems. Just like us. Everyone has problems. Theirs happen to be mental. If you understand them and what they are dealing with, you no longer have any desire to call them *crazy*, a label that isolates them.

I chose to understand them, and I chose to help them.

Generally, that help took the form of aiding them in living in the world they had created in a way that allowed them to function as happily as they could without causing trouble for anyone else. I did not try to cure them, just as I could not cure someone who is paralyzed from a spinal injury. What I could do was help them negotiate the world. I looked for practical solutions to deal with the problems as they existed, not to make the problems go away.

I remember a young man who really lived in "another world" and believed he was a bulldozer. Unfortunately for him, others did not see it that way. He went down to a construction site in the middle of a big intersection on a busy road and started doing what bulldozers do: picking up loads and pushing piles of dirt around. People stopped him, and he was picked up by the police. In his mind, though, they were stopping him from doing his job.

When I got involved with his case, I realized it would be useless to try to convince him that he was not a bulldozer. That was the world in which he lived, and he was not going to move. So I decided that to keep him safe and happy, we had to change his worksite. The young man saw things in mirrors that did not appear to him on blank walls. So we put a large mirror in his room and then, at his request, a second one. Those mirrors reflected a work site to him and with their help he was able to do his bulldozer job in his room all day long. He was extremely happy with this solution, and it stopped him from going outside looking for work to do.

Another time, I treated a girl who had, in addition to lot of other problems, severe obsessive-compulsive disorder. She decided that all the television sets in her unit—there were three or four of them—had to be turned to channel five. Naturally, this caused chaos with the other patients who would be happily watching something on another station when she barged in and changed the channel. Again, I could not help her to overcome her problem, but I could alleviate the situation.

I managed to persuade her that every time she walked into a room, instead of putting the TV on channel five, she had to sit in a reclining chair and adjust it and lock it five times. This was much easier for her to do, and it did not affect the other patients. It was a solution that worked for everyone.

I once met a patient I'll call "Jerry," who had an invisible friend named Fred. The two of them would carry on conversations and argue. Several times, the staff of the hospital got Jerry a job, but it would not be long before he was fired. The arguments he was constantly having with Fred were too much for the people around him to handle.

When Jerry came to see me, I let him talk to Fred for a little while, and then I told him that I was only going to treat Jerry and Fred had to leave. I got up, held the door, and insisted that I wanted to be alone with Jerry. Jerry, astonished to learn that I could not see Fred, very reluctantly allowed Fred to wait outside. Eventually, I got him comfortable with spending less and less time with Fred. I convinced Jerry that he should leave Fred home when he went to work because other people could not see him either, and it bothered them.

It sounds like a silly solution to the problem, but it was a practical one and it worked.

In one of the first psychiatric centres where I worked, I met a forty-seven-year-old woman who had problems putting things into a sequence. If she needed to go to the washroom, comb her hair, and call her mother, she did not know which to do first. Then she would become frustrated, start yelling, throw things, and occasionally break things.

This had been going on for many years when I met her. I talked to her and studied her place in the hospital carefully before coming up with a simple plan that involved her and her caregivers. When she started to feel frustrated, she was to start slowly counting out loud—"One, two, three, four . . ." When the staff heard her counting, they were to immediately intervene and tell her, to use the above example, that she had to 1) comb her hair, 2) go to the washroom, and 3) call her mother, in that order.

This worked out quite well. She liked the new way of doing things and did not get so frustrated, but it only worked for a while. About six months later, I was in the caregivers' station, which was not far from her room, and I heard her unhappily counting: "Fucking one hundred and one, fucking one hundred and two, fucking one hundred and three," and so on.

It was funny, but sad. While she had followed my plan, the staff had stopped paying attention to her unless she broke something or caused some other kind of trouble. It was a case of the squeaky wheel getting greased. Unfortunately, that is common in our society. I tried to explain to the staff how important the plan was, but they smiled and shrugged and said: "You're right, but . . ." That is human nature.

A lot of people end up in psychiatric hospitals because they feel safe there; they are not being criticized or stared at. Many do not belong there, even though they have been there most of their adult lives, but it is a haven for them—sometimes the only one they can find. When I worked in a psychiatric hospital, I became fascinated with the worlds these people inhabited, with the reality they had constructed. When I can find a way to understand the world that these problem-wracked people live in, then I can find a way to help them to be happy. That way might not include a cure, but it does include understanding and compassion.

ARE WE ENTITLED TO ENTITLEMENT?

ONCE UPON A time, I was on a plane and had to go to the bathroom—again, no surprise there. I was sitting near the front, right behind business class, and there was a toilet quite close to me that no one was using. Nonetheless, because I was not flying business class, I was forced to walk all the way to the back of the plane to pee. As a society, we accept that some people have more privileges than others—that some people on planes, who have paid more for their ticket, will enjoy bigger seats, better food and drinks, and a toilet they do not have to line up for.

Do they deserve this? Are they entitled to these privileges? Is it their right? This is something I have thought long and hard about, not just regarding something as relatively minor as a plane ride, but in our everyday lives. What are rights and privileges and how do we come by them?

I think we have certain rights. They include the right to live our own life, the right to freedom, the right to choose, the right to freedom of expression, the right to love, the right to our own feelings, the right to learn, and the right to earn, and so on.

A teacher who had lived in both underdeveloped and developed countries once told me that the difference between the two was that in developed countries your rights are given to you, and in underdeveloped countries you must fight for them. When do our rights and entitlements match, and when do we become entitled beyond our rights? This is a problem in our world.

I think you have the right to things by earning them, but you are not entitled to have them without earning them. So, what is the meaning of entitlement?

Dr. John Townsend, in his book *The Entitlement Cure* (Zondervan 2015), defined entitlement as two beliefs: first *I am exempt from responsibility* and second *I am owed special treatment*. In other words, if someone has a sense of entitlement, they believe they deserve certain privileges and are arrogant about it.

In my practice, I have seen repeatedly how a sense of entitlement can cause sadness and depression. Patients have sincerely complained to me with such grievances as these:

> *"I am thirty years old. I should have a permanent job."*
>
> *At my age, I should have my family established."*
>
> *"My father worked hard, so I deserve a better life."*
>
> *"I deserve to have a car."*
>
> *"I am old. People should respect me."*
>
> *"I am a woman, and men should respect me and give me what I want."*
>
> *"My spouse should always tell me where they are and stay in constant contact. I am entitled to know and will be upset if I find out later that I haven't been told something."*

There are many more examples, but these illustrate the point.

I think we have all run into entitled children and adolescents. A lot of them feel entitled to get whatever they want. I have seen adolescents with this sense of entitlement and then seen them again as adults. They were depressed and hurt because the world had not given them what they thought they deserved.

Not long ago, I saw a woman who believed she deserved to get whatever she wanted. I told her she had the right to whatever she desired, but she needed to work for it. Intellectually she understood what I meant, but inside she felt nostalgic for the munificence of childhood, when she received everything she wanted because her parents gave it to her, and she thought this should continue throughout her life.

I talked to my son, who has three small children, about this. We agreed that as parents, it is nice to provide a great life for children, but they need to learn not to be unreasonably entitled. They need to have chores, to learn to help others, and to wait their turn if necessary. They need to have an allowance, to learn to save and to spend, and to sometimes give without any expectation of receiving.

A lot of people like to receive and do not like to give. I am sure most of us have seen people who are like that, and it is not just material things that they are acquisitive about. They also feel they deserve positive feedback and compliments without any responsibility for paying such things in return. Yet most of the literature on this subject reports that life is much better for people without entitlement syndrome.

I encourage people to take inventory of their own entitlements: material objects, respect, title, privilege, and extra perks, and see if they are mixing up their rights with entitlement. Knowing your rights is hard and understanding what you are reasonably entitled to is even harder, but it makes for a better person.

III

Tune-Ups for
Relationships

NOT ALONE IN BEING LONELY

I LOVE CONNECTING with people. I have always been able to make both social connections and friends. Being interested in others and reaching out to them has helped me throughout my life. It has certainly eased the transitions as I moved from one country to another. However, if I have something bothering me and I am not ready to talk about it, I feel lonely.

If I can feel lonely, then anyone can. Whether we want to admit it, or not, we all feel lonely sometimes.

A few years ago, I met an older gay man who had never come out of the closet or had an intimate relationship. He'd had a good working life doing something he enjoyed, but now he was retired and was getting more and more depressed, despite the fact that he had plenty of money, lots of time, and no particular stress in his life.

He had been shy as a child, and his parents and older brother had been at best cold and uncommunicative and at worst verbally abusive and critical. When these factors were added to his sexual orientation, which was much riskier to reveal in that less-inclusive time, his life had pretty much been lived in isolation.

When he came to see me, it was the first time he had ever sought help for what was a classic case of loneliness. Although the path he trod was unique, there are many ways people can become lonely.

I have seen or heard of people experiencing loneliness for the following reasons: being in a new place; being in a situation or place where the other people are different, which is not necessarily the same as being in a new place; having no intimate attachments or relationships; having no time for oneself; not being able to trust anyone; being a quiet person; having a disability; not knowing the language; keeping a secret that does not allow openness; being in the habit of keeping to oneself; and having a grim or unwelcoming face or expression.

These are just some examples. I am sure there are many more.

When I was young and living in my homeland of Iran, if someone asked me what my name was, I would say "Khalili." I felt I was part of the Khalili identity, part of a group, a member of "us." I belonged. We were all like that. We all had a feeling of belonging. Even walking into a strange place, we would say "Hello, Brother" or "Hello, Sister" to make an instant connection, whether there was someone else there or not.

In North America, however, when asked the same question, most people are likely to respond with their first name, because individual identity is given more weight and promoted more extensively. I think this emphasis on individuality and privacy leads to loneliness by creating barriers between people. In fact, it is commonly reported that 50 per cent of North Americans feel lonely, a higher number than is found in eastern countries.

Human connection is extremely important to us, whether we realize it or not. If we are feeling lonely when we are confronted by stress, challenges, and bad feelings, our bodies and our brains must use more resources to meet the challenges and confront the sources of stress. In fact, homesickness, a common kind of loneliness when we miss the life and people we were comfortable with, is a known mental health problem like depression. We need one another.

The power of human connection has been a central focus of the Virginia Affective Neuroscience (VAN) Laboratory at the University of Virginia. Dr. James Coan, a psychology professor and the director of the lab, uses neuroimaging such as EEGs and fMRIs to study brain plasticity and social relationships. He reports that there is real potential for preventing and treating a wide variety of medical and psychological maladies through social relationships.

Clearly, overcoming loneliness is particularly important. How do we recognize that we are lonely? How do we recognize loneliness in others? What can we do about it?

It is easy to recognize what we need physically. For good health, our diet should contain enough (but not too much) food, with a certain degree of variety. We should consume liquids, vegetables, fruit, dairy products, grains, and meats in balance. That is easy to recognize, but our social health requires similar balance. If we know ourselves well, we can recognize that we are lonely and we can figure out what is missing from our social diet. We need to be understood, validated, and connected with a variety of people. If we are not, we are probably lonely. Most animals are the same way.

How do we go about curing our loneliness? There are many steps.

First, we need to get enough (but not too much) sleep. Sleep problems and loneliness may be related. I once had a patient who would sleep whenever his partner was gone. He would sleep from eight o'clock at night until eight o'clock in the morning because his partner worked nights. I told him to stay up later, which forced him to interact with others and keep himself busy. As a result, he felt much better personally and much better connected to the world.

We need to take a good, hard look in the mirror—not to see how many wrinkles we are getting or how fat our cheeks have become, but to check the expression on our face. Do we have an open face, ready to smile? Does our gaze veer away from meeting others? A closed, forbidding face can discourage others from making initial contact or reacting positively when we reach out.

The COVID-19 pandemic has taught us the importance of socialization and human connection, because following the rules put forth by our medical experts necessarily left many people isolated and disconnected. This was an unusual and unfortunate circumstance. In "normal" times, is it important for our well-being to connect.

We need to learn to greet people. This morning as I was walking along, I saw at least eight people. To each of them I said: "Hello!" or "Good morning!" and about half of them answered back. The ones who do not respond are likely to be the loneliest. We must try to connect with people on the most casual level with neutral ("hello") or positive ("what a beautiful day") comments.

Stay open to others while in a holding pattern. Recently I went to see my urologist. I looked at the people in the waiting room and more than half of them were lost in their own worlds even while sitting right next to each other. We need to be present and enjoy these moments, whether we are waiting for a doctor or a plane or our turn at the grocery checkout. Learn to open up.

It is a good component of a social diet.

We need to nurture each other by lending a hand when necessary, making a positive comment or smiling. One day I was at a large grocery store and a woman needed help getting an item off the shelf. Five people stepped forward to lend assistance, and everyone felt better afterwards.

Do not be too judgmental about others and do try to see more positive things. For example, people come to see me professionally because there is something wrong. Nonetheless, I also look for something right with them and bring it to their attention.

Do not dwell on rejection and the way people respond to you. This is quite common. If you do not get the job, look forward to getting the next one, and if people are negative, that is their problem, not yours. Do not make a big issue of it. I once had a patient who complained because people always looked at her because she wore a hajib. I asked her why she was focussing on that. She knew it would happen and needed to just deal with it, to get over it, not to fret about it.

Finally, avoid ruminating. Ruminating is going over the same thought or problem without solving anything. As I said earlier, do not have a dirty mind. That just leads to depression and anxiety.

So what did I tell my patient who had never had a long-term relationship and was lonely? "You have ten or twenty years left. How do you want to spend them? Make a plan."

THE HILLS ARE ALIVE WITH THE SOUND OF MUSIC (AND SWEARING!)

AS MENTIONED EARLIER, when I was a young boy, my family owned a pomegranate orchard. During the spring and summer, out in the country at our farm, I would spend hours and hours walking through the pomegranate trees. There was something about walking through nature that simply dissolved all my tiredness and stress. Those pomegranate trees are long gone, and I live thousands of kilometres away from my homeland, but I still walk and hike through trees and bushes whenever I get the opportunity.

I am no Forrest Gump, but some studies suggest our earliest ancestors would travel as many as twenty-five kilometres a day hunting and gathering food. Maybe that is why keeping moving, specifically in my case walking, seems to come so naturally.

When I first moved to St. John's, we lived in a house right next to Bowring Park, a beautiful and expansive green space in the city. Day in and day out I walked through this wonderful place, going farther and farther every time. Mostly I walked by myself, but I was often joined by my son, Sammy.

Eventually, I met other people who also enjoyed walking and hiking. Over time, we started our very own hiking group. First, there's John, who I call "Johnny." He is tall and younger and loves to jump into and swim in any kind of water—salt or fresh, cold or not. There is Pat, a family doctor whose daughter was a friend and classmate of my daughter. It was our children who brought us together since we both loved hiking. There is another John (John C.) and another Pat, whom I'll call "Paddy," Jim, Sandy, and Dan. Although not everyone has gone on every hike and some people have moved on over the years, this is what I consider our core group.

In 2007, my son and I asked Pat if he would like to join us in hiking the Inca Trail to Machu Picchu, the world-famous archaeological site in Peru. Thus began a tradition that we have been carrying on ever since.

Shortly after our trip to Peru, we decided to go on a long hike in our own province. Naturally, we went looking for a challenge and decided on the Long-Range Traverse hike in Gros Morne National Park, located on the west coast of Newfoundland. The mountains there rise straight up out of the water. It is not a climb for sissies.

We invited a few other friends who gladly accepted and one summer morning at six-thirty, we set off, seven of us in two cars, to drive the seven hundred kilometres to the park. The excitement and joking around started almost immediately and lasted all through the day. We arrived at our cabin in the park about four p.m. Beer and sunshine contributed to keeping our spirits high. We had been waiting for this moment for quite some time.

The next day we set off on our hike. Only nine people a day are allowed on this hike, and we had registered, paid our fees, and been given an orientation lecture when we arrived. We were also outfitted with an electronic monitor to track our movements in case something was amiss. There was no cellphone coverage in the mountains, and the park rangers wanted to be able to find us if necessary.

We had to take a taxi, a three-kilometre hike, and a one-hour boat ride down Western Brook Pond before we even got to the start of our four-day trek. (What we call a pond in Newfoundland would count as a lake anywhere else.) Finally, the boat dropped us off at the end of the pond, and we were ready to begin. You must be an avid hiker to take this on. The trail stretches for 36 kilometres, reaches 1,581 metres high, and is rated difficult. If that were not enough of a challenge, we were each carrying fifty-pound backpacks containing everything we would need, and we were climbing straight up with no clear path. It was quite an introduction to the land.

About half an hour in, Frank, another beloved member of our group (who has since moved on to heaven), fell and injured his hand. Fortunately, no bones were broken, as Pat, our resident physician, assured him. Twice I fell off the path and rolled over a few times while wearing my heavy pack. I was pronounced fit to carry on. We were quite a loud group, calling and talking and, yes, swearing, as we climbed up and up. It was as wild and untamed as Jurassic Park up there, but with bears and moose instead of dinosaurs. Everyone looked after themselves, but at the same time we watched out for each other and helped when necessary. If there was a hidden danger, like a hole in the ground, someone would yell out to warn the others.

One of the first things we learned to curse was tuckamore, which are stunted trees that grow almost horizontally in the harsh winds of Newfoundland. This underbrush makes finding a path much more difficult and travelling it even harder. "No more tuckamore"—with a judiciously inserted swear word in the middle—soon became our mantra. In fact, we now call ourselves the "No More Tuckamore" group.

We started out walking in close formation, but it did not take long to realize that we had a scout in our midst. Paddy would slowly get farther and farther ahead and then come back to tell us what the path before us was like. He was not the only one who developed a specialty. Dan became our navigator and compass reader, since we did not have coverage for a GPS or phone. I can still hear him yelling out, "Soon we will see a large body of water on our left."

The hike was quite strenuous, but by five p.m., after a long climb and a five- or six-kilometre hike, we arrived at our first campsite. Even though it was the middle of summer, at night it got quite cold—four or five degrees Celsius. We were not allowed to have a campfire, so we had to cook our food on a small, portable gas stove. But at least we had made it.

The next day we carried on. We got lost and took the wrong path several times—if you could call them paths. After an hour or so, Dan or Paddy would get us sorted out and find the right route. The mountain was gorgeous, and the men continued to be positive and fun to be with.

That evening I began my role as entertainment director. As we gathered in one of the tents, I initiated a game of "When was the first time?" I asked people to talk about their first day of school or first failure or first kiss: whatever we could think of. It loosened us up quite a bit, and we became closer as we shared our experiences at the top of a mountain in the middle of that splendid nowhere.

By the third day, I could tell that the men had really bonded. We accepted each other's strengths and weaknesses and enjoyed each other's company and sense of humour. I felt I really belonged to a group and that they accepted me for who I am—it was a powerful and positive feeling.

On the fourth day, we arrived at the other side of Gros Morne. The view was breathtaking. We were both happy and sad. Happy to be almost finished this long hike and sad because this joyful experience was coming to an end. Even now, when I look at the picture of us at the bottom of the mountain, I can see the joy (and weariness) on our faces.

Thirteen years later, we are still a very tight group. We have bonded more and hiked even more. Although not everyone has been able to make every trip, we have gone all over the world together, from Europe to Africa to the tip of South America and Antarctica. We all know each other's weaknesses, and everyone has a role they play. I love every minute we are together. There is no pressure, just acceptance. Everyone helps each other to appreciate nature without damaging it, and every experience is a positive one. Even when tuckamore is involved.

When you are out in nature, people are just people. There are no politics, no professions, no jockeying for position. No one is the boss. You have only one purpose and everyone shares that purpose and helps each other. That is why the group is still together and why we leave our spouses and our children behind to share this special connection.

Male bonding is necessary for most men because the genders are simply different. Spending an occasional few days together with members of your own sex and doing something healthy is a good thing that can never be replaced by any other joy.

Except maybe finding a place to hike where there is no tuckamore!

ON TOP OF THE WORLD AT THE BOTTOM OF THE EARTH

M Y HOMETOWN, QOM, is on the boundary of the Central Desert (*Kavir-e Markazi*), about 140 kilometres south of Iran's capital, Tehran. It is quite flat there and extremely hot, often climbing above forty-five degrees Celsius in July. Summers are long and winters are short. When I was a young boy studying geography in school, I learned that we were in the middle of the world and there was a North Pole above us and a South Pole below us. In any pictures I saw, these places were always white, cold-looking, and extremely far away.

Because I was a dreamer, I wanted someday to see and walk on the top and the bottom of the earth. When I moved to Canada and settled in Newfoundland, the weather was so different from what I grew up with that the pictures became real to me, even though I was not actually at one of the poles.

In 2011, my buddy Pat suggested hiking in Antarctica. Johnny jumped at the idea, and I let my old wish to walk on the bottom of the earth come to the surface again. We decided to go for it and were joined by Pat's friend Sandy, whose sense of humour and positive attitude made him a good addition to the group.

It turns out that getting to the bottom of the world is quite complicated and entailed several stops along the way, including in Santiago, Chile. We stayed there three days, and I found it a beautiful and well-organized city with very friendly people. I have never been to a place where people were so nice to stray dogs. It was dog heaven.

We spent our time there having a mini vacation before the real fun began. I saw the statue of former president Salvador Allende, a democratic socialist, next to the main government building. I saw one of the famous Café Con Piernas (coffee with legs) coffee shops, where the waitresses wear miniskirts and high heels, which is considered quite risqué there. We did not go in. The Chilean food was delicious, especially the cheeseburger I ate in a small café. We went to a beach on the Pacific Ocean on a Fun Bus and visited a famous vineyard.

Then, finally, it was on to Argentina and Ushuaia, the most southerly city in the world. Oddly enough, Ushuaia has a similar climate and landscape to St. John's, which is also on one of the four most extreme points of the Americas—it is the most easterly city in North America. From there, we boarded a boat to take us across the Southern Ocean to Antarctica.

The ship we were on had once been a research vessel and held about a hundred and ten passengers and thirty crew members. It was not exactly luxurious. I can still see the tiny cabin I shared with Johnny. There was only about three feet between the small bunk bed and the bathroom door. We had to share the bathroom with Pat and Sandy, who were next door in an equally small room.

We set sail at about four o'clock in the afternoon, and sometime after midnight, we entered the rough-and-tumble South Polar Ocean. (Earlier in this book, I shared the story of the fear that gripped me on this high-seas adventure.) After about fifty hours of sailing, we got our first sight of Antarctica. The fifth-largest continent has a land mass of fourteen million square kilometres blanketed by an ice sheet that holds 60 to 90 per cent of the world's fresh water. It has no indigenous population and is governed by international treaty. No one owns the land, and no humans live there permanently, although about five thousand people work there at different scientific stations.

But that does not mean it is empty. There are seven species of penguins inhabiting the continent and six species of seals. Whales patrol the surrounding ocean, and forty-six species of birds, including the albatross with its three-metre wingspan, call Antarctica home. There is no vegetation.

I have never been so far from a cream puff in my life.

For the next week, we moved to a different part of Antarctica every day. We were there in February, which is summertime in the southern half of the world. The temperature hovered between about minus five and minus ten Celsius, but it was sunny and bright. Each day after breakfast, we put on our boots and our life jackets and got in the Zodiac, which would take us to land where we could hike.

We hiked up the hills to see the penguin colonies. What a beautiful sight, and what an awful smell! Penguins are fascinating birds and are quite hilarious. They walk a couple of kilometres from their hill down to the ocean to feed and to pick up small stones to build their nests. It was funny to see how they stole stones from each other (although probably not for the penguin who had trudged all that way to get the stone in the first place) and how they treated their babies.

The penguins chased the krill, the seals chased the penguins, and the whales chased the seals. This game of survival went on constantly.

The sense of isolation is profound. The biggest sound you hear is that of the icebergs cracking off into the water. One day, I was the first to reach the top of a hill. I had a moment of spirituality—the sun was shining, and as far as I could see there was only white snow and blue water. It was a perfect picture and completely quiet. I stood there thanking God for allowing me to have the means to travel to this place and enjoy such beauty.

Suddenly, I heard a voice behind me declare, "Life is good, ain't it! Life is good!" Sandy had come up behind me. We sat together and admired the beauty all around us.

Another day, we had the opportunity to take an "Arctic Plunge." Johnny was one of the first ones to jump into the icy water next to an iceberg. When I asked him how he felt he replied, "When you hit the water it feels like you are being hit hard with a hard object."

He survived. I did not try it.

One evening around eight o'clock, the Zodiac dropped several of us off to spend the night on the ice. We had to dig a "grave" in the snow for insulation and put our sleeping bags in it. Because it was summertime at the southern end of the Earth, the sun did not really set; it was still light out. We could see quite well, so before we tucked in, we played minigolf on the snow with red plastic balls. That night we slept quite close to the seals, and we could hear and see where the icebergs and mountain ice were breaking down.

A trip to Antarctica had always been on my list, but I am not the only one. It is quite a common entry, not just for scientists and academics, but for adventurers and hobbyists as well. I am probably on the adventurers' list. Our trip there and back again from the south of Argentina took about eleven days, and during that time we met people from all around the world. They were a select group who had the physical fitness and financial wherewithal to be able to add spice to their lives by making such a trip. Once again, I met some nice people and some weird ones. I was proud of our own small group, proud of how we presented ourselves as travellers who appreciate nature and other people and are fun and respectful. I thought we represented Newfoundland well.

On our return trip to Canada, we stayed for a few days in Buenos Aires, a gorgeous city. It was a joy to visit the fine restaurants where we encountered friendly people, some of the best beef I have ever tasted, and fine wines. One day we took a ferry across to Uruguay. Another day, Pat and I visited the famous La Recoleta Cemetery to see the grave of Eva Peron, the first lady of Argentina, who before her death in 1952 at the age of thirty-three, was given the title "Spiritual Leader of the Nation." When I arrived home after my trip to the very end of the earth and back again, I was engulfed by a feeling of accomplishment and satisfaction. I had visited a place of perfect cleanliness, sublimely pristine in its beauty. I also felt close to the countries I visited and the people

I met on the journey.

Visiting Antarctica changed my life and left me with a feeling of great satisfaction. My reality and the imagination of my childhood came closer together. That journey expanded the cream puff world in my mind, and it remains to this day a beautiful memory.

CONFLICT AND RESOLUTION

A WHILE AGO, a couple came to see me for a "tune-up and oil change." They had seen me several times in the past and now were just checking in to keep the engine of their marriage running smoothly. However, one hour soon turned into two as I realized the conflict between them related to past relationships that had not yet been resolved.

In the beginning, as their relationship formed, and later, when it looked as if they were becoming a permanent couple, they dealt with their other intimate relationships each in their own way. One cut off all contact and the other maintained friendly interactions. Neither of them liked the way the other had handled it.

I normally look at things from a psychological point of view to unearth the causes of conflict. I examine how each person processes information, how each one's needs, fears, and values are impacted, and what skills they have used to deal with the problem—such as communication, problem solving, or decision making.

When an action that has already caused conflict is repeated, it not only causes hurt and distrust, it makes the conflict grow. In the case of many couples, it reaches the point where they leave the relationship because they cannot resolve the problem. That is what was building up in this couple's relationship.

Yet if the conflict can be dealt with in a smart way, significant progress can be made. Look at our parliamentary system, for example. We have a government, and we have a shadow government—the opposition. That opposition, pointing out problems, makes the issue clearer. Conflict, in this instance, becomes a good thing, leading to a better outcome.

It is not just couples (or governments) that need to learn to deal successfully with conflict. I have provided conflict resolution in workplaces throughout my career. I use testing and interviews to look for and assess the following causes of conflict: unfair treatment; unclear job roles; poor communication; poor training; poor work environment (such as excessive noise or overcrowding); unequal opportunities or pay; harassment or bullying; personality clashes; too many changes in the organization in too short a time; unrealistic needs; unrealistic expectations; unresolved conflicts; increased workloads; and conflict of values. There could be other reasons as well, such as cultural differences, poor management strategies, and racial conflict.

Typically, we respond to conflict, either in the workplace or in our personal life, by avoidance, fighting, or reluctantly giving in. All these strategies yield short-term solutions, but they never resolve the real point of conflict. That takes understanding, compromise, and collaboration and, quite often, bringing in someone who specializes in conflict resolution. This will result in a better outcome.

Sometimes conflict occurs within ourselves. That is a little different. We cannot avoid, fight, or give in to ourselves. Yet internal conflict is quite common and can come in several forms. First, the conflict may be between two good choices, such as whether to go to an Italian restaurant or an Indian restaurant, or to wear the blue dress or the red one. It's surprising how much turmoil some people feel making this sort of decision. The conflict can be between a good outcome and a bad outcome, like someone who does not like people choosing whether to become a lighthouse keeper or a social worker. This seems like a no-brainer, but occasionally I see patients who have given in to other pressures and chosen what seems an obviously wrong choice for them. In doing so, they have made a long-term commitment to conflict.

The conflict is between two unwanted results, such as going the long way around or climbing very steep steps to get to your destination when you are already very tired.

But no matter whether the conflict is within oneself, with another person, with work, with nature, or with life itself, it is good to learn strategies to resolve it. There are certain basic steps I run through when I am resolving a conflict of my own.

Conflict Resolution Checklist

- [ ] While acknowledging my feelings, am I using my intellect to solve the problem?
- [ ] Is it necessary to validate my feelings? Or is the conflict too complicated because really, two duelling emotions are at play?
- [ ] Am I using emotional reasoning and believing something is true regardless of the evidence?
- [ ] Am I realistic? Am I being honest with myself?
- [ ] Is the issue worth the aggravation?
- [ ] Are my values being too compromised?
- [ ] Do I have enough information?

☐ *Did I genuinely hear and understand the other side of the conflict?*

☐ *Am I clear about what the issues and other factors are?*

Many of these questions overlap, but if the answers are generally yes, then I am ready to decide. It is important to note that the decision might not be perfect, but it is the right choice for me at this time.

For example, I had a friend for many years who used the worst language. I did not mind it when we were younger, but later, when I had small children, I did not want him to swear in front of them. I warned him that in my house, we did not speak like that, but he would not listen and continued in his usual way. Finally, I made the decision to break off our friendship. I was sorry, but I felt I had made the right decision. It was a conflict of values, and I saw no other path.

Another time, I relied on a friend to put some money I had given him into my bank account, and instead he kept it. It was a lot of money, but when confronted he seemed deeply sorry and was quite upset. I had to decide whether that money was worth our friendship because I knew I would never get it back. If he had acted belligerently or confrontationally when I confronted him, things might have turned out differently, but because of his repentance I decided to retain our friendship (although I will never trust him with money again).

In both cases, I used the checklist to make my decision.

Regardless of whether the conflict is within myself or with an outside party, I use the information with the idea of coming to a resolution—whatever it might be. I do not allow avoidance, fighting, or giving in to play a part; instead, I rely on compromise and communication.

This is the strategy I used with the couple who had differing ideas about maintaining old relationships after they became a couple. I ended up speaking with each separately and going through the list. This helped them clarify their positions. They agreed to behave in a certain way, and that settled down the conflict they were going through.

Conflict is not a bad thing. It makes things clearer. It gives people the opportunity to learn about each other and grow their relationships, but it must be resolved. If conflict is resolved successfully, then the relationship becomes even stronger.

TRUST

I RECENTLY RETURNED from a vacation in Florida. It entailed four flights—two to get there and two to get back home again. I had the choice of a few airlines, but I flew with Air Canada even though I knew there was a good chance their flights would not be on time. In fact, Air Canada only manages to reach its destination in a timely manner about two-thirds of the time, and that is an average. Some months, there are many more delayed flights than that. Sure enough, my expectations panned out. Half of our flights were delayed—one until the next day. I was not surprised.

Why would I choose an airline with such a poor record when it comes to getting me from one gate to the next in a reasonable amount of time? Because I have confidence in its ability to get me from one gate to the another, even if it does not do so in a timely manner. Air Canada has a seven-star safety rating and is one of the top twenty safest airlines in the world. I trust Air Canada to get me there and back again safely, and that is more important to me than getting there and back again on time, every time.

In fact, my whole life is based on trust. Trust is intrinsic to every aspect of our existence. When I drive down the street, I trust that the car coming towards me will not veer into my path. When I go to a restaurant, I trust that the food has been prepared properly and hygienically. When I make a purchase, I trust the brand name of the product. I even trust the government—although I am not naïve about the shenanigans they get up to, I have faith in the process.

Trust plays a huge role in my practice. Before I can begin to help anyone, two issues need to be addressed. First, I need to trust in my skill and my knowledge and my ability to help this new patient. I can do this because my confidence in my knowledge and skills is not static. Even though I have been doing this job for over forty years, I do not just rest on my laurels. I continue reading the latest professional and academic journals; I attend seminars and conferences; I listen to what other experts in the field have to say, and I listen to and learn from my patients. All these things contribute to my confidence in my own ability. If I did not continue to do these things, my trust would not match reality. Rather, it would be an unwarranted belief.

I remember being in court about ten years ago to testify as an expert witness. The other lawyer was trying to discredit me. He kept asking how many MMPIs (Minnesota Multiphasic Personality Inventory) I had administered. The MMPI is a famous and popular standardized test of adult personality and psychopathology. I told him I had done it hundreds of times, but the lawyer would not accept that.

"How many hundreds?" he asked, as if the absolute number mattered. "Eight hundred and forty-two?"

How can anyone say how many tests are the right number of tests? A test is a test. I had enough confidence in my abilities to remain unflustered. In my own mind, I knew the value of the test and exactly how much it was able to tell me. Without that trust in myself, I would not have been able to respond appropriately. I relied on my own ability, and he could not shake that trust.

The other issue that needs to be addressed before I can begin to help someone is their attitude. To benefit from my help, a person who comes to see me has to be willing to trust me with their issues. If they do not, we cannot make any progress. Trust on both sides means we can create an open and relaxed environment that allows positive progress to happen. From the beginning of the first interview with a new patient, I am assessing what that person needs in order to trust the process and to trust me to guide them through successful therapy to meet their goals.

All this trust is based on solid information. It is not unthinking adherence to a belief system. People or businesses are trusted when they consistently do things properly. That is why it is such a blow when trust is broken, which happens when someone involved does something wrong, either deliberately or by accident. To build someone's trust in us back up involves committing to showing our feelings, admitting we made a mistake, and learning not to do it again.

I had a patient once who cheated on his wife. He sincerely loved her, and he regretted what he had done, but the trust in their relationship was broken. He was willing to do whatever it took to rebuild it. It took a lot. I helped him devise a plan that entailed calling his wife often and telling her exactly where he would be whenever he was away. Yet every time he had to be out of touch, when he was on a job that took him out of cellphone range, for example, she believed he was with another woman. Perhaps while I was telling him all the things he needed to do to regain her trust, she had a psychologist coaching her not to open herself back up to heartbreak. I would not be surprised. Broken trust is extremely hard to mend.

To truly trust another person and have them trust you in return requires what I think of as the four Cs:

1. **Connection**—A person has a certain something that gives you the motivation to invest in the relationship in the first place.

2. **Consistency**—You need to know what you are saying, walk the walk and talk the talk, as they say. You need to be consistent: keep your promises, keep the other person's secrets, share your feelings, and admit your mistakes.

3. **Commitment**—It's important to be honest about the degree of commitment you are willing to extend and then honour it.

4. **Courage**—Relationships take faith, because life is messy.

This sounds difficult, but in real life it is a lack of trust that causes most of our anxieties. Anxiety and fear are really the result of a lack of trust, either in the world around us or in ourselves.

It can get extremely complicated. Take erectile dysfunction, for example. Men may turn to medication when the problem could be psychological. They forget that an erection and sexual arousal are not the same thing, and they put their trust in the medication because they have lost trust in their own bodies.

The other day, a young woman told me that she did not trust

herself around men. When I asked why, she said that she was abused several times by different men she had been in relationships with. She said, "I do not trust myself, and I do not trust men, but I do not trust myself more."

Yet she could not tell me what it was about herself that she did not trust. She had many problems, but it was her self-distrust that she emphasized. She needed to figure out what she was doing so she could stop and begin the journey towards trusting herself again.

Building trust is hard and losing it is easy. To trust ourselves, we need to take an inventory of what is right about ourselves. This can include our knowledge, our skills, our strengths, our value system, our belief system, and our personality—what we like and what we love.

We also need an inventory of both our successes and our failures. We should not just dwell on our failures. We need to learn from them.

So I asked the young woman to monitor herself and recognize when she got to the part of herself that she did not trust. I told her to be clear. She lacked knowledge about herself, and she needed to learn what, for example, she liked about men and what she needed to have a stable relationship.

I have come up with a simple checklist illustrating the indicators that tell us we can trust someone in a relationship.

The Trust Checklist

Trust someone who will

☐ *share all their feelings*

☐ *admit when they are wrong*

☐ *share details of their lives without hesitation*

- [ ] *share their financial information and their finances*
- [ ] *go out of their way to put you at ease*
- [ ] *drop everything to talk to you, let you talk, ask questions without making it feel like an interrogation, hand over the phone without hesitating, and hold natural, genuine conversations*

Trust is a two-way street. To be trustworthy one must
- keep promises, keep secrets (of the other person, not from the other person)
- communicate openly
- not be judgmental
- allow vulnerability
- forgive
- disagree in private—be supportive

Working on a relationship based on trust, each partner must
- share mutual values
- foster kindness
- allow the other person space
- show love
- make the other person and the relationship a priority
- stay to the end

We trust that our plane will get us where we want to go safely. We trust that our food contains no harmful or inappropriate ingredients and will nourish us. We trust that we can share a bed and sleep soundly at night. It is what makes the world go round.

Trust me on that.

SARCASM—IT'S NOT FUNNY

W HAT IS EMPATHY? The *APA Dictionary of Psychology* defines it as "understanding a person from his or her frame of reference rather than one's own, or vicariously experiencing the person's feelings, perceptions, and thoughts."[5] That sounds like a good thing to me—something we should all cultivate.

What is the opposite of empathy? One definition is callousness: not feeling or showing any concern about the problems or suffering of other people. I believe that this opposite force working against empathy can often manifest itself as sarcasm.

The *Canadian Oxford Dictionary*, 2nd edition, defines sarcasm as "the use of bitter or wounding, especially ironic remarks." It does not always have to be verbal, although it usually is. It can take a more physical expression—eye rolling, elaborate shrugs, smirking, even just ignoring what a person has just said or done.

Many years ago, I had a co-worker who was an expert at sarcasm. The other people in the office called him the whippersnapper. I did not like the kinds of remarks he used to make, and I never laughed at his so-called humour. He acted as if he were smart and funny, but his behaviour caused him to become more and more isolated. When I look back, I realize that I did not like him. I do not know where he is now, but I assume he is a lonely man.

As you probably realize by now, I do not like sarcasm.

I see it a lot in my practice, especially between couples. They say things like:

"Yes, you were just trying to help her."

---

[5] VandenBos, G. R. (Ed.). (2007). APA Dictionary of Psychology. American Psychological Association.

"I know she's 'just a friend.'"

"Yes, you were too tired. I understand."

"Oh, you are a very hard worker. You are not lazy at all."

"Poor you."

"I understand. It's not your fault at all."

All these statements are the exact opposite of what the speaker really means, and they are designed to demean the other person and reduce their credibility. As soon as a sarcastic remark is made during a session, I put a stop to it immediately.

People who are emotionally mature never use sarcasm because they never want to hurt anyone. So why do some people use sarcasm? I think sarcastic people do not like themselves very much and so they project that feeling onto others. It is also a way to distance themselves from others—and that certainly works. People who are the butt of sarcasm feel very alone. Not only that, deep down inside, a part of them agrees with what the sarcastic person has said about them. That makes the whole thing worse.

Sarcasm hurts. It damages a person's self-esteem and sense of self-worth and makes them feel insecure. It can cause anger and provoke a feeling of vengeance, as well as a feeling of being bullied and manipulated. It erodes trust and intimacy between people and can damage and even break relationships. Once the damage has been done, the hurt feeling does not go away. I know this. I have heard it from my patients, and I have felt it myself.

I cannot figure out what the benefit is to this kind of behaviour. Sometimes it is just a bad habit, and it is more common in some cultures than others. I think some people do not even realize how harmful it is, but I believe it should be stopped.

I think parents and even friends should educate people about sarcasm. On a regular basis in my practice, I remind and educate my patients of the harm sarcasm causes, but I also teach them how to deal with it—how to minimize the damage it causes. I am not the only one to come up with a solution. Some self-help literature indicates, to some degree, the same approach.

While I do not agree with any use of sarcasm, I think it is important to recognize and distinguish between sarcasm that is meant to be hurtful and sarcasm that is simply playful. The first is, of course, more serious.

There are two important points to remember. First, sarcasm is simply bad behaviour and second, we can learn to minimize the damage it causes us when we are on the receiving end.

Try to understand it for what it is and do not give it too much weight or meaning. Try to let it slide off your back. Treat it like a noise. We can all learn to ignore certain noises, even if they are very irritating. Sarcastic noises can be treated the same way. Taking a different approach, you can be assertive and tell the person what you felt. However, do not demand they understand what they have done. There may be other options. Perhaps you can find them for yourself.

We cannot expect empathy from everyone we meet. However, we do not have to take its opposite so much to heart.

A FRIEND INDEED

I ONCE SAW a man whose wife of twenty-five years had left him for the third time, and now she wanted to come back home. In the past, he had always agreed, but now he was asking me for advice. I told him I thought he should move on with his life and not keep making the same mistake—but I bet he allowed his wife to come back once more.

This encounter made me think about marriage, and also about friendship. There are some couples in the world who are married, but they are not friends.

That led me to wonder, what *exactly* is friendship?

A famous Persian poet from the thirteenth century whose work is still revered today, Rumi, once wrote about friendship. He said:

> I love my friends
> neither with my heart nor with my mind.
> Just in case . . .
> Heart might stop.
> Mind can forget.
> I love them with my soul.
> Soul never stops or forgets.

Rumi also said there are three kinds of friends in the world. The first are the ones who only want something from you—bread friends. His suggestion was to give them what they want—feed them, and then let them go. They have nothing to offer you.

The second kind is the talking friend, someone you want to spend time with. This is a friend you respect and keep and whose company you enjoy.

The third type is the best kind. That is the soul friend. You give them part of yourself, part of your soul, and they are with you forever.

Many years ago I saw a research article comparing Iranian and American friendships and the way the people of these two different cultures see friendship. Americans were reported to be very practical. They would say something like, "Bob and I are friends because we play baseball and drink beer together." If for some reason the two stop playing baseball or drinking beer (or being neighbours or working together), then the friendship comes to an end. When Iranians say they are friends, they remain friends, even if they do not see each other much or no longer do things together.

I started wondering if this were true and decided to ask the people around me what friendship meant to them. I asked my wife, my children, my friends, and my colleagues. Here are some of the responses I received:

> *Trust: when I am with my friend, I do not watch my back.*
>
> *I can depend on them when I am in need.*
>
> *I am myself with my friend; I am at ease; I enjoy spending time with them; I am happy with them; I am not judged.*
>
> *I am accepted as I am; I feel I am liked; I feel I am supported.*
>
> *I want to care about them; I am interested in their life.*
>
> *When I am having a good time, I wish my friend were with me.*

The meaning of friendship is very individual. People look at it from their own perspective. It was interesting to see that most people spoke of the benefits they received from friendship rather than what they offered. "I" was at the centre of most of their responses, and maybe that is a good thing. Many people propose that having great friendships is better for our health than quitting smoking, improving our diet, and exercising.

I honestly believe this to be true. Having good friends contributes a great deal to our health and happiness. However, each of us has different views on this as well, as different needs for friendship. The more schizoid a personality you have,[6] for example, the less need you have for friends because your world is so much smaller.

Yet even people who acknowledge the importance of friendship often have difficulty making friends. I remember talking with my children when they were growing up about how to make friends. This is something we do not really learn in North America.

How do we make friends, and then how do we keep them? I think we need to work at it, just as we work at other important things in our lives. Friends deserve the investment of time and energy it takes. So, this is my list of how to keep a friendship healthy: call and visit your friends; be part of the events in their lives—the good times and the bad times; be good to them; do not do anything that would hurt them; and praise them whenever you can.

How many times have you run into someone at a store or restaurant and bemoaned how long it is been since you have seen each other? You are sincerely sorry, but neither of you has done anything about it. You say you will get together soon, and you really mean it. But do you do it? I spend at least one or two hours every single week keeping in touch with my friends because it is necessary to maintain those friendships. It is a great skill to have and to hone.

I must confess it has become a little easier to maintain my friendships as I grow older. When I turned fifty, I decided it was time to stop always being the one who made all the effort. Until then, I had called people and I had visited people. I wanted to see who would be left if I no longer did that and I think 80 per cent

---

[6] Schizoid personalities live in their own bubble and do not feel the need to interact with others.

of my friends dropped out of my life. But really, they are no loss. Now, I still have talking friends aplenty and a small group of soul friends I will always treasure.

Friendships are not always equal, of course, even between two people. A person can be an A+ friend to you and you can be only a C- friend to them. That is not a good thing; it is something else we should work on repairing. We need to have A+ friendships on both sides of the equation, and if we do not care enough to put in the effort, we should not be surprised if that friendship fades.

Friendship can also change. I have a friend with whom I have been close for many years. Now he has Alzheimer's and no longer knows me. I struggle with understanding what my responsibility is to him.

No one said friendship is easy, but it is worthwhile.

As for my patient with the wandering wife, he really had no idea whether he and his wife were friends or not. He obviously had difficulty understanding the meaning of friendship. He needs to learn how to be a friend and how to find a friend. That will make all the difference.

LEARNING NOT TO BITE

AS I HAVE mentioned before, I have been going to the gym at six o'clock in the morning for many years. That is how I have managed to stay in shape for all the hiking I do, as well as for day-to-day life. There is a man at my gym who works out at the same early hour. He has been doing so for about twenty years.

I am an agreeable guy. I nod and smile at people when I pass them by. I make small talk with strangers in the grocery line.

I think pleasantries are the lubricant that keeps the wheels of social interaction moving smoothly. So for the first few years I would say "Good morning" or "Hello" when I ran into this fellow early-morning fitness buff. He acknowledged my greeting, but not once did he ever initiate an interaction. Given the opportunity, he completely ignored not only my existence, but that of any other people who were around. He did not have a clinical or psychological problem. He just did not read social cues.

You know what? This behaviour drove me around the bend. It's not just that I didn't like it. That's fine—I do not have to like the way other people behave. But I did not like the way it stayed with me. It was like he was holding out a hook, and I wanted to bite it—hard.

American statesman Thomas Jefferson once said, "Do not bite at the bait of pleasure, till you know there is no hook beneath it." Biting in anger is the same thing.

Almost all of us communicate with each other verbally, but we also communicate using body language. I understand what you are saying by taking my cues from your words *and* from your physical actions, and you do the same thing. We often convey the wrong message. We do not mean to. It is just that we have not learned how to communicate emotionally. This is one of the reasons they invented emojis to go along with our social media messages.

So the guy at the gym got to me. His emotional communication (or lack of it) frustrated me, and he probably did not even realize it.

But sometimes people do realize it and they do it anyway. They are trying to get people to bite. I see that when married couples come in for counselling.

When people come to see me, there are often two different
factors that need to be dealt with. The first one is the actual problem
or problems they are having—perhaps their values conflict or they
have different mindsets.

The second factor is their emotional communication. To figure
out what needs to be done with the underlying problem, I need
to recognize some of the ways they communicate emotionally. I
study their body language—whether they look (or don't look) at
the other person, whether they keep their distance or stay within
close proximity, whether their arms and hands are relaxed or look
ready to strike, and what kind of expression they have on their
face: smiling, smirking, angry . . .

I also pay attention to their choice of words. The words
people use can be kind or mean. If you call someone "cheap," it
comes across as quite different from calling them "thrifty," even
though the two words mean essentially the same thing. How
people phrase things is especially important.

The tone of voice they use is also important, as is the volume.
I pay attention to whether someone is speaking very loudly or
in a normal voice, and I listen to what I call the music of the
voice. That conveys the mood and attitude of the person speaking
and will directly affect the impression it makes on the person
who hears it. These are all aspects of what we call paraverbal
communication.

A couple who came to see me recently had become experts
at the most damaging kind of paraverbal communication. They
had been baiting each other for three years. By that I mean they
were deliberately trying to elicit either an angry or an emotional
response from each other.

There are many ways to do this. These include making an

accusation seemingly out of nowhere, demanding something, playing on the other person's emotions, deliberately making the other person jealous, and acting like the perpetual victim.

With this couple, it was difficult to tell which one was the fisher and which one was the fish. In fact, they each played both roles and were able to bait each other by attacking the most sensitive areas and biting down. That just escalates the fight, which is why they needed me to help put a stop to it.

Often, this kind of problem arises in people who are highly intelligent. The wife in this instance was very smart and seemed to think she knew everything. She was five kilometres ahead of everyone else, tapping her foot impatiently while waiting for them to catch up, and as a result she stopped listening, not just to her husband, but to me as well.

I finally had to ask her what she thought I was there for, if she was always so many steps ahead of me. She needed to slow down, stop rolling her eyes, and listen to what I had to say. Even though she thought she knew where the conversation was going, she did not, really. She needed to stop baiting both of us. And she did eventually, after many hours of persuasive therapy helped her gain insight into her own behaviour.

It was a hard lesson to learn, to stop baiting, but the couple realized it was the only road they could take that would lead to healing their marriage.

Just as crucial as not baiting is not biting.

Five years ago, I met a hockey coach who had a couple of kids on his team who misbehaved. He was pretty firm in correcting their behaviour, and it happened that one of the miscreants was an only child with an overprotective mother. She rushed to her baby's defence and emotionally beat up on the coach so badly that he ended up quitting. Many years later, the incident still bothered him.

He had done nothing wrong, but the mother baited him, just as she had probably baited many other authority figures in her child's life, and he bit. He failed to realize that he is not a fish!

We must choose not to bite. We must choose not to rise to the bait. One way to do this is to recognize when another person is baiting us. It is like advertising. It is not a coincidence that snack food commercials start turning up on the TV around eight o'clock in the evening. If we do not recognize what the advertisers are doing, we take the bait and trot into the kitchen for something to eat. Once we recognize that they are trying to manipulate us, it is much easier to stop that automatic response.

So, even though I did not like the way the guy in the gym acted, I eventually learned to shrug it off. He behaves the way he behaves. That is just the way he is. I do not have to take the bait. I choose not to bite.

I have even learned not to get annoyed when people ask me where I am "really" from.

I admit it does not always work. I still occasionally bite if someone questions my integrity or my professional competence. This is something that is important to me, and it is hard not to take the bait.

Nonetheless, I am a human being, not a sockeye salmon, and for the most part, instead of biting, I force myself to swim . . . I mean walk . . . right past that hook, no matter how tempting the bait.

"DO AS I SAY, NOT AS I DO!"

THIS IS AN admonition parents have been handing down for generations, and its antecedents go back almost as far as written language. We generally see it as something quite hypocritical. Children are being told to act in a certain manner even though the advice is not being followed by the very person giving it.

It can be interpreted in another way as well. The statement seems hypocritical because the listener discounts it. To the person being spoken to, the important part of the interaction is not what is said. In fact, that is the least important part of the message.

According to George J. Thompson, who wrote the book *Verbal Judo: The Gentle Art of Persuasion*, there are three elements of communication. First, there is the truth—what someone says. This accounts for about seven to ten per cent of the importance of the message as far as the listener is concerned.

Next comes the voice—the way the words are spoken. Voice has four elements. The first of these is the tone, which indicates the true attitude of the speaker. I remember once working on something during a flight and running out of paper. I very politely asked the flight attendant if she might, by any chance, have a couple of sheets of paper I could use. Her response made me feel terrible. She looked at me coldly and said, "We do not carry those things, sir. Sorry." But because of her tone of voice, what I heard was, "Sit down and shut up."

Other elements of voice are pace (how fast the person is speaking); pitch (how loudly or softly they are speaking); and modulation (the rhythm and inflection of their voice).

We use these elements all the time, almost automatically. When you are trying to calm a crying baby, you do not yell at it to shut up. You speak gently and soothingly. Our voices and how we use them carry a lot more weight—thirty to forty per cent of the message—than what we say.

That is why when we are told to "Do as I say, not as I do," we discount the words and use the person's actions as our guide, whether it is right to do so or not.

This is a central aspect of emotional communication. I believe we communicate with each other in three important ways: verbally, physically, and emotionally. The first two are relatively easy to understand. When someone says "Pass the salt," you know what to do. It is just as clear what you should do when someone holds the door open, which is a physical communication. However, emotional communication, which has also been called effective communication, active listening, and mindful communication, is a little more difficult. It goes beyond the fundamentals of strictly conveying information and instructions.

I once had a meeting with a forty-five-year-old woman who was strong-minded and well-spoken. Four years earlier, her husband had died in an industrial accident. Unfortunately, she saw the autopsy report and it traumatized her. Even after all that time, she could not get the picture out of her mind. That is why she came to me.

She sat in my office and talked about her work and her home and other things in detail, but she did not talk about how she felt. Occasionally while she spoke, tears would run down her cheeks. Yet she continued to speak as coolly as she could about the details of her day-to-day life.

She even went into the details of losing her husband in a matter-of-fact manner. However, I could tell there were a lot of emotions bottled up inside her that needed to come out. She seemed to be stuck in the first, second, and third stages of grief.[7]

---

[7] Stage one: my loss is not real; stage two: my loss is real; stage three: I must adjust to the new reality; and stage four: reinvestment in life.

Her family and friends, as well as her common sense, kept telling her to let go and move on, but she just could not bring herself to do it. I tried to listen to her feelings as well as what she said, and then I asked her if she was ready to let go. She told me she did not want to let go; she was afraid of feeling empty and alone. She knew her husband was gone, but she wanted to stay in the same place emotionally.

I was able to draw this out of her because I listened to her emotional communication. Had I simply heard her words, I might have thought she was fine, but what she was saying and what she was communicating emotionally were two different things.

What I was doing was actively listening. Active listening involves really hearing what the other person is saying and paying one hundred per cent attention to them. It is not judging and it is not preparing an answer for when the person stops talking, which is what most people do after hearing a couple of sentences.

When you actively listen, you can then rephrase, summarize, and identify the feelings the other person has shared. And you can confirm that you have truly understood correctly. I do this with my patients all the time. When they open up to me, I will respond with some variation on "You said X really bothered you. Are you still upset by it?" or "This event brought back other memories. Am I correct?"

An active listener responds by showing they have heard what is being said. They do not respond with some sort of solution to something they have decided is the problem. They do not respond with a conclusion or a verdict. Because the person who is speaking is trying to deliver a message as they understand it, and that can be a struggle. Restating what has been said and asking if you have it right helps the speaker to complete that message.

This comes up all the time in couple's therapy. I had a couple come to see me who had been fighting for years. She was trying to get him to hear what she had to say. "Please listen to me!" was the message she was trying to convey. However, he kept correcting her as she spoke. He was not listening to her. He was inserting his version of the story without ever hearing hers.

Part of the problem is that we all have things that are emotionally important to us, but are not necessarily important to someone else, or at least not as important to someone else as they are to us. For example, I have a few things I am very emotionally invested in: my views on friendship and love, my quest for acceptance, and my homeland. When I talk about any of these things, it is really on an emotional basis. It is my heart that is speaking, not my head. If the person I am speaking to only listens to my words, they are missing most of the message. To me, the feeling I am trying to convey is the most important part of what I am saying, and to only listen intellectually minimizes my feelings. The whole conversation becomes derailed.

That is what happens to many couples. Communication becomes derailed because they are approaching the same event in a different way. For example, something happens and one person begins to cry. She is responding on an emotional level and revealing her feelings. Her wife, on the other hand, reacts to the same occurrence on a rational, intellectual plane. This happens because she does not understand the depth of her spouse's emotional commitment to the issue.

I like to get them to list the issues that are close to their heart and then discuss that list with each other. When each person understands and respects the issues that the other deems important, they can truly communicate. The speaker feels safe and supported, and the listener can actively and emotionally contribute.

As for the couple who had been fighting for four years, I was able to teach the man how to truly listen to his wife. During individual sessions, I taught him to hear the emotion behind what she was saying, to acknowledge and validate it, and then to wait until she told him she was ready to hear the explanation. He became more intelligent as a result—emotionally intelligent. Life is much easier if we are skillful in emotional communication.

So do as I say—and as I do.

TRUTH, LIES, AND WHAT LIES BETWEEN

IMAGINE YOU ARE in a fancy restaurant having dinner with a friend. You have just finished the main course and your friend has ordered something luscious for dessert. You are trying to cut down on calories, so are simply enjoying a cup of coffee after the meal—but, man, does that dessert look good! Your friend, seeing the look on your face and knowing you well, holds out a forkful and asks if you would like a bite. "Oh, no!" you exclaim, after the briefest hesitation, "I am full."

A few weeks later, you are in the grocery store stocking up on supplies. You've been home with a migraine for a couple days and the cupboard is bare, so you have dragged yourself out despite not feeling well. You run into the same friend, who asks cheerfully, "How are you?" "Oh, I'm fine," you automatically respond, despite the pounding in your head.

You are such a liar. We all are. Lies are the salt and sugar we sprinkle on our social interactions to make them taste better. Life would be a lot more difficult if we told the truth all the time. Think how self-conscious your friend in the first paragraph would feel about eating dessert if you explained that you really wanted some too, but had to practise a little willpower, and let's be honest, no one really wants to hear the minutiae of our health issues, especially in the produce aisle. So we tell these little white lies and things go more smoothly because of it.

As we know, too much salt and sugar in your diet is not good. Their overconsumption leads to diabetes, high blood pressure, obesity, and all kinds of other health problems. Lying is the same. Too much can cause problems.

More than thirty years ago, a family came to me for help because one of them had gone well beyond what we might consider "acceptable" social lying. They owned a successful business; everyone contributed and was good at their job. However, it came to light that one of the daughters was stealing from the business. After this was discovered, her husband disclosed that she also told lies—a lot of lies. This led her mother to admit that as a child her daughter had told a lot of lies as well. They wanted me to help her stop her dishonest ways.

Once people start lying routinely, it is like putting too much sugar in your coffee—exceedingly difficult to stop. Lies grow and grow and the gulf between the lies and the truth grows wider and wider, necessitating more lies. Cheating is a member of the same club. Malingering, for example, is a case where a person fabricates or exaggerates symptoms of illness or injury to gain a financial reward or to escape responsibility and guilt. In that case, lying and cheating are virtually identical.

When I first met with their daughter on her own and asked why she had come to see me, her response was that she had been caught lying and was told to come to therapy. She agreed—reluctantly. She had insight into her behaviour and why her family would be concerned; however, she was not fully committed to honesty.

What did I do?

I introduced her to the concept of radical honesty. This is a behaviour management plan that involves absolutely no lying whatsoever. Not to yourself and not to anyone else. One hundred per cent honesty, always. Radical honesty is as difficult to achieve as quitting smoking or stopping drinking or breaking any of those other bad habits that are so tough to renounce. In fact, it may be harder. Someone who commits to radical honesty has to "wear" their monitor all the time. Nothing can be said, no question can be answered, without screening the response for complete veracity.

The cure was in her own hands. As I explained to her, she was in control of her healing. To help her, though, I always insisted that she had to be completely honest with me, even if she slipped with others. I asked her to keep a record of every urge and every lie. I also enlisted the help of her husband to be my assistant. His role was to monitor the amount of lying in between sessions and keep a log. Both agreed to this process.

At the end of a week she was exhausted. Then I discovered she had also been smoking and hiding it from everybody, including her husband. She finally admitted to smoking, since it was no longer pleasurable, as it involved too much hiding.

In a few weeks she had become skillful at the game of lying—she would tell a lie, call it truth, and then tell the truth and call it a lie.

In the next couple of sessions, we dealt with issues of respect, shame, and confidence, and adjusted her goals. Her husband was good, but tired. Fortunately, she was able to gain some insight into her weaknesses and strengths and eventually internalized what she wanted, which was to be normal and healthy. This was a major step because she had entered therapy only half-heartedly.

When we were done, the business books were finally cleared, her husband had become more positive, and her parents were happy. I held a final family meeting, and we drew up an aftercare plan of dos and don'ts. I think it was a successful intervention.

There are many ways we lie to ourselves and to each other. One type of lying is not telling the truth by keeping quiet when we know about something that happened. Unfortunately, we see this a lot in our society. Someone sees a friend's husband out with another woman and does not say anything to his wife. Or a person knows who cheated on their income tax or who put the dent in a neighbour's car and keeps quiet about it. I have seen that kind of silence cause shame and guilt later on.

Another way to lie involves making up stories to be entertaining to others or to help build one's own ego. Many, many years ago, an old cousin of mine told us a story about how he caught a rabbit while he was riding his horse. As kids we were extremely impressed. As I grew older, I heard the same story several times, but the rabbit became a fox and then a deer and then a wolf, and my cousin sped along in pursuit from an initial twenty kilometres an hour to one hundred kilometres an hour (what an amazing horse!). The story grew with every retelling, becoming a bigger and bigger lie.

Perhaps that one was harmless in the great scheme of things, but lying can exact a cost. I think the worst form of lying is lying to ourselves, because eventually our grasp of reality becomes blurry. It is something we do more often than we realize. It takes the form of making excuses for the events in our lives. We tell ourselves things like "I missed doing my exercises today because

I was too tired" or "I did not get a good grade because the teacher did not like me" or "I ate all the chips because I was really hungry." We know deep down that these excuses are not true, but we tell ourselves these lies anyway.

This kind of lying happens a lot in my practice. For example, some of my patients lie about how bad or how good they feel. How can I help them if that is the case? I try extremely hard to mark the boundaries of our relationship in terms of what a session can and cannot provide. The more I understand the psychology of the lies I am told, the more skeptical I become about my ability to help.

So, practically speaking, how do we deal with lies in everyday life when they go beyond little white lies? Should we confront them or not? That is the million-dollar question. I have several criteria I follow, depending on the situation. If the person I think is lying is close to me, I need to deal with it, so I ask a direct or indirect question to clear the air—and I keep asking questions if necessary. If the issue is not important or the person is not someone I am close to, I must decide whether to pursue the issue on a case-by-case basis. However, if there is potential for someone to be harmed, or if it is a question of criminal behaviour, I find a way to confront them. However, I would not use salty language or sugar-coat it. That is not healthy.

THE MARRIAGE GARDEN

SOME YEARS AGO, a couple came to see me. They were a professional couple in their fifties with four children who were, for the most part, doing well. However, they were having difficulty with one son, and they wanted help to figure out how to deal with him. It was obvious from the start that the woman was the spokesperson for the pair. She explained everything and answered all the questions, even though I was addressing them both equally. Finally, I turned directly to the man and told him I wanted to hear his side of the story. As I spoke, he seemed to clam up, and his eyes widened in distress. Immediately, his wife pulled her chair closer to his and took his hand in hers. She turned to me and said, with no fear or reticence, "Dr. Khalili, you have hurt my husband's feelings."

At this point I knew, and I told the couple so, that their relationship would last forever, no matter what problem they were having with their son. I saw them many years later and they were just the same. They always would be.

How did I know their relationship was so strong? Because of the way the woman responded when it appeared her husband was in distress. She had no thought but to protect him. I had caused him suffering and she was springing to his defence. That is the definition of a good marriage, one where one partner can see when the other needs care and provides it.

I envision everyone as being partly adult and partly child. The child lives inside and is protected from the outside world by the adult. In a successful marriage, the two inner children like each other. They enjoy playing with each other. They are relaxed with each other. Their defences are down, and they fully accept who the other person is and are accepted for who they are in return.

The adult sides of the pair form a protective barrier around the inner children, like a fence around a garden. Inside the garden the children are free to be themselves, to share with each other, to grow a stronger and stronger bond. They can do this because the adults are there to deal with the outside world and protect the children inside. This can only happen if they let their guard down and trust the other adult.

The complete acceptance of the inner child on the part of the adult is key. If one adult starts criticizing the other's inner child, starts taking control and acting like a parent trying to mould the inner child rather than accepting him or her, then the barriers are raised, and trust is lost. If that happens, the marriage simply becomes a contract between two adults who have agreed to share their lives together.

And after all, why do we get married? Is it to have children and financial security? Or is it to become whole, to be part of something better? If it is the former, marriage is an obligation. If it is the latter, it is a true communion.

It is like the relationship between grandparents and grand-children. They connect in a special way. I have grandchildren whom I love dearly, but they do not see me as a parental figure, and I do not act like a parent with them, except to the extent of making sure they come to no harm. When they see me, they take me by the hand and ask me to play. They fully accept me for who I am, and I fully accept them for who they are, without any criticism. We both like each other and love each other.

Marital partners need to strive for the same relationship. Protected by the adult outside, the children inside can play in the garden, growing flowers together, not pointing out weeds.

There should be a big sign on the wall formed by the adults saying "No Parents Allowed!"

BAD APPLES AND HAPPILY-EVER-AFTERS

PEOPLE CONSTANTLY ASK me how to go about finding the "right" partner and vice versa—how to avoid getting involved with the "wrong" partner. I am not surprised. Finding Mr. or Ms. Right and avoiding Mr. or Ms. Wrong is one of the most important things we do in life. To make a good choice, we need to be clear on what we want and what we don't want in a partner.

Of course, no one is perfect, and no one is totally imperfect either. We need to strike a balance, or better yet, tip the scale towards the good side. Think about running into someone you know at the grocery store. Almost the first thing you say is "How are you?" Some people shrug and answer "Not bad," as if that were a good thing. That is not true. "Not bad" is not the same as "good." There is a long continuum that runs from awfully bad through bad, not good, not bad, and good to very good. Why settle for not bad when there are all kinds of better options?

It is the same with relationships, only they matter a lot more than a casual conversation you have while you are lined up at the checkout counter.

When you are standing in the produce section looking over all the apples, you have a lot of decisions to make. First, you must decide what kind of apple you want (some like them tart and crisp, others prefer sweet and soft), how much you can afford to pay (imported Granny Smiths cost a lot more than domestic McIntoshes), and finally which apple in the category you have selected you are going to pick. I think everybody chooses the same way at this point. They want something clean and shiny, without any bruises or bad spots.

How do you pick a partner with no bad spots and bruises? Well, that's probably impossible.

It is possible, however, to find a partner with fewer bad spots, and we can also look for certain traits. These are some of the things I consider bad spots in a prospective partner. Beware of someone who behaves in these ways:

1. is emotionally needy
2. is emotionally reactive
3. is self-absorbed, self-centred, or narcissistic (all about themselves)
4. is impolite or rude to others
5. practises poor self-care (clothes, teeth, general look)
6. is not any fun to be with
7. lacks empathy for others
8. thinks of themselves as a victim
9. reacts angrily to feedback
10. is closed to new experiences
11. is not comfortable with different opinions
12. oversteps boundaries
13. is deceptive
14. tries to manipulate you or others
15. misunderstands too much (they "don't get it" too often)
16. focuses too much on the negative
17. is a bully, shows controlling behaviour, or is punishing
18. is contemptuous/only sees the negative in you
19. is paranoid
20. is jealous

21. is a heavy drinker or dependent on mind-altering drugs

22. has a lot of toxic relationships with others

23. is habitually not punctual

24. is not present emotionally

25. makes aggressive remarks often

26. wants to move much faster than you do in the relationship

27. talks excessively about their ex

That is a long list.

We need to be good at detecting these bad spots and digging to find out more. For example, someone whose emotional response is extraordinarily strong—they get hurt quickly or angry easily, or they're rude to other people or very negative—probably has other bad spots as well. That might not be a relationship you wish to pursue.

Unfortunately, when we meet someone we are attracted to, we may choose to ignore the warning signs, but at least we can recognize them.

The other side of the coin—how to find the right partner, not just avoid the wrong one—may also be helped by a list. Here are good qualities to look for—the rosy, unblemished bits of the apple.

Those good qualities are found in people who behave in the following ways:

1. They look straight into your eyes and give you genuine attention.

2. They are mature and emotionally present.

3. They conduct themselves with integrity.

4. They are self-confident and honest, have a strong identity, and present themselves well.

5. They have a positive attitude.

6. They value commitment.

7. They are polite, respectful, considerate, and attentive to others.

8. You feel relaxed, energized, and happy to be with them—they make you smile.

9. They listen intently and seek knowledge.

10. They are willing, friendly, and do not gossip.

11. They are observant and kind with everybody.

12. They do not rush you.

13. They are open-minded.

14. They are comfortable in conversation.

15. They are aware of others' needs.

16. They're stable emotionally, economically, and intellectually.

17. They looks groomed and have good hygiene.

18. They appreciate and understand love.

19. They show respect for the environment and nature.

20. They respect your opinions and beliefs.

That is also a long list!

It is important to realize that these are all qualities we should strive for in ourselves, as well as in a partner. We must remember we are not the only one going through the apple bin. We must present a polished, unbruised appearance to someone seeking a partner.

I examine this a lot with couples who have come to see me with relationship issues. Many of them have lost some of their good qualities and have acquired some bad traits such as jealousy, mistrust, and lack of communication. If we do not correct our own bad spots, and we continue to fight with our partner about it, we both become undesirable, the way one apple can spoil another one close to it.

To begin polishing your own image, go down the list and ask yourself, "Am I like that?" If you find a black spot, clean it. It is a good, mature strategy, and it helps in the quest to find the right partner or to be a better partner.

Unlike apples in the grocery store, we can change. We can make the bruises disappear. We can shine.

THE "BUT" STOPS HERE

GOATS MUST BE the most disagreeable animals in the world. No matter what you say to them, their heads go down and they have only one answer. Butt. That is offensive, don't you think? It means that no matter what you say, the goat already has his answer prepared and is not going to listen.

Now maybe I'm exaggerating about goats. I am sure if you offer them something to munch on, like a piece of kale or an old tire, they will give a completely different answer. However, I am serious about that response to everything else. As soon as you get "but" as a reaction to what you are saying, it means the other person has already decided not to listen. They have already formulated an answer.

I think I hear "but" more than the average person does. Maybe a lot more. I am in the business of talk therapy. Talking things out to come to resolution is what I do. Yet it seems that every time I try to correct a statement based on errors in thinking, I immediately get "but" thrown back at me. "But I was angry." "But I didn't mean it.""But it isn't fair." But, but, but. Just like a goat.

These people are not listening to me. They have not heard what I said. I can tell because they are not acknowledging the possibility that they could be wrong. By using the word "but," they are already arguing. They are not thinking about my words. They are responding automatically.

I had a couple come to my office once whose marriage was in trouble. The woman had found some texts on her husband's phone that were obviously inappropriate. He had been carrying on a flirty conversation with a co-worker. He saw it as completely innocuous. His wife, however, saw it differently.

The wife was not wrong. He should not have had that conversation, even though he said it did not mean anything. However, she cranked it up way farther than it needed to be taken. It was a relatively small problem in a long marriage. What I saw was a rash growing on the skin of their relationship, something that had to be treated so things would be better. She saw cancer or heart disease or something of the most profound seriousness. She would not listen to my diagnosis, and I could tell because the answer to whatever I said to her started the same way.

Our conversation went something like this:

> Me: *Your husband seems to have done a lot already to make it up to you.*
> Her: *But not enough.*
> Me: *He sincerely apologized.*
> Her: *But you do not know him as well as I do, and his apology does not mean much.*

Me: Try to give it a chance.

Her: But if I give it a chance, I will be disappointed again.

But, but, but to everything I said. How futile. This could have gone on forever.

It was something she did all the time in many circumstances. It was a way for her to focus blame and it was also how she justified contradicting what the other person had just said. An English teacher would describe "but" as a conjunction that indicates that the next clause will contradict the previous one in the first clause of the sentence. By using "but" in conversation or in an argument, we are actually saying that the other person is wrong and, further, that they are not worth listening to. By doing this we cling to the belief that we are right. That is what the wife in this case was doing.

I think we have a habit of using "but" as a way to bring a conversation to an end. We block the other person's statement with a "but" to stop them from speaking and ourselves from having to hear. It is very dismissive.

This causes two problems. First, we are not actively listening, which means listening with your head and your heart, clarifying and rephrasing if necessary, so that you fully understand both the other person's point and their feelings. With active listening, a conversation can continue rather than be derailed.

The second problem is that by saying "but," we do not learn from the perspective of the other person. It does not matter if the perspective is right or wrong. We can still learn from it.

It took a few hours, a few sessions, until I finally got the wife in this example to listen to me. I had to stop her both from physically saying "but" and also from thinking it.

In the end, the husband learned he could not overstep the boundaries the way he had done, and the wife learned that she had a responsibility to him—she needed to stop saying "but" and actively listen without judging. As a result, their relationship improved. They both stopped saying "but" all the time in response to what the other had to say. They were able to set themselves and their own feelings and arguments aside long enough to listen to each other.

Sometimes the thing the person is fighting against is true or could possibly come to pass. It is like a person who is afraid of flying. If you tell them they will be fine, they will respond, "but the plane might crash!" And they are right. However, the plane might not crash. The plane most likely will not crash. We do not know the future. We should not use "but" to stop ourselves from living.

Imagine that goat no longer responding to everything with a "butt." He may discover that life is surprisingly good when he is no longer smashing his head against everything.

By eliminating "but," you too can stop smashing your head against everything and improve your life.

iv

The
Contentment Cake

THE CONTENTS OF CONTENTMENT

"Now is the winter of our discontent / made glorious summer by this sun of York."

That is the opening line to William Shakespeare's historical play *Richard III*. If only it were that simple—a little bit of sunshine, a touch of summer—and suddenly all our discontent is swept away. Of course, we'd still have real winter to deal with, but Shakespeare's Duke of Gloucester was speaking metaphorically.

So, can we make all our discontent go away? Can we become content by deliberately deciding that is how we want to be? By an act of will? I think so—but we must work at it. Most patients come to me because they are discontented and unhappy. The ultimate goal of therapy is to help them become content and happy. If it were easy to do, they would not need me! But how do we do it? How do we make ourselves content and happy?

First, we need to decide what we mean when we use terms like contentment and happiness, and we must realize that they are not the same thing. The main difference is that happiness is temporary. You go out for dinner with friends and the food is good and the company is good, and that makes you happy. Someone gives you a gift you really like, and that makes you happy. You land a new job, you ace an exam, your daughter is coming home for Christmas. All these things make you happy. Happiness is living in and enjoying the moment. It is a temporary mood tied to something specific.

Contentment? That is more difficult to define. It is a more permanent state of being. Dictionaries define contentment as peaceful satisfaction and freedom from worry or restlessness. Have you ever watched a baby sleep? If that baby is warm and fed, it can literally sleep without a care in the world. All its needs have been met. It is utterly content. The same is true of our pets. If their needs are met, they are worry-free. Can you imagine a cat lying in bed at night worrying and unable to sleep because it does not live up to its own expectations? Because it thinks it should be smarter or prettier or more self-confident? Me either.

We are not cats, and we are no longer babies. Our lives are not so simple. There is no going back to that state. Our intelligence will not allow it. We think too much and as we grow, we are dealing with an increasingly complicated world. We have no choice. So, how do we achieve their level of contentment? How do we free ourselves from worry and gain peaceful satisfaction? We must become content with our lives.

I have spent many years listening to my patients, reading scholarly articles, and listening to experts so that I can understand how to become content. It took many years, but finally I have come up with a list of ingredients to bake a "Contentment Cake."

The first ingredient is self-acceptance. Remember the cat with no self-doubt or criticism? This is the heart of contentment—to accept ourselves as who we are, not who we think we should be. We must accept our bodies, our looks, our race, our sex, our background, our age, everything about ourselves. This is who we are. One of the first things I do with a patient is ask them to do a self-image test. They usually find out that they do not accept themselves as they are. Some do not even like their own name! But this is something we must overcome. You do not have to be a good person to accept yourself as you are. You just have to be at peace—at peace with your flaws as well as your good points.

The second ingredient is to have a positive outlook towards the world. I am not saying ignore the bad things. I am not saying ignore hardship. They exist. You cannot deny that, but we can focus on the good. There is a lot of negativity in the world. We see it daily in the news, and we hear it from others. Yet there are people in the world who have experienced many hardships but still manage to maintain a positive outlook. I recently had lunch with a former patient of mine who is seventy-eight years old. She has had all kinds of problems in her life, but her spirit shines through. She is a role model and pleasure to be with. She has learned to develop a positive outlook.

The third thing we must do is recognize that the locus of control is within us. There is nothing that can push me into a negative state, nothing that can make me anxious or angry or depressed, unless I allow it. It does not matter what it is. We are the captains of our own ships. Your mother cannot make you miserable. Your son cannot make you miserable. Your boss cannot make you miserable. Those things are all external. Allowing yourself to become miserable is something you do to yourself on the inside.

Think about the phrase, "You make me so mad!" We have all said it, but it is not true. The "you" in this sentence has said or done something, and you have allowed yourself to get angry about it.

To use another example, imagine your small child is having a temper tantrum and shouts, "I do not love you anymore!" Now imagine your spouse quietly says the same thing. What a different reaction you experience to the same words. You have filtered and interpreted what they said and formulated your own reaction. They did not do that for you.

Recognizing that we are in control of our emotions is not the same as being happy all the time. It is okay to cry at a funeral, but we must use our intelligence to overcome our problems and worries, and then stop worrying when the problem goes away. Babies cry when they are hungry, but they stop when they have been fed. They have returned to a content state.

The fourth ingredient to add to the Contentment Cake is being open to learning. Continually upgrade your knowledge and understanding. Never stop reading, listening, watching, and reflecting. Think of discontentment as being like a bad smell. If you smell something bad, you try to learn what is causing it and you try to fix it. You address the problem; you do not ignore it. If you cannot repair it, if the smell is coming from someone else's drain, you have to recognize that you can only do so much and learn to live with it. Do not complain and then ignore the problem.

That used to be all I thought we needed to live a contented life, but a few years ago I realized there was another ingredient that helped me a great deal. That is to nurture your spirit by being close to nature. This can be on the smallest scale, and it does not mean that you must drop everything and go forest bathing. A patient once gave me a small tree, not much bigger than my hand, for Christmas. (I learned later that it was a Norfolk pine.) It purified the air in my office and was my friend for several years. Eventually it needed more space and we moved it to a church in Mount Pearl. Then I grew a lemon tree, which was about two inches tall when I received it as a gift and is now brushing the ceiling. This constant connection with a piece of nature in the unnatural surroundings of my office helps me to feel contentment every day I am at work. And I hope it also brings some temporary happiness to my patients.

SELF-ESTEEM: IT'S ALL ABOUT "ME"

WHEN I LOOK into a mirror, I see five of "me" looking back. We all do. No, this mirror is not in a fun house, and there is nothing wrong with my vision. So why do I see almost half a dozen of me in the mirror? Who are these reflections?

First, there is the real me; then there is the me I think I am; there is the me I tell myself I should be; there is the me I want to be; and finally there is the me I fantasize about being. That is a lot of me!

Let us break them down.

The real me is the person I am. To give a physical example, I am five feet, six inches tall. There is no changing that. It is not bad or good. It is a fact. It just is.

The second reflection is who I think I am. This is where judgment starts to appear. I can have an opinion about this me— and I do! This is the me that says, "I am short" or "I am tall" or "I am medium- sized." This is the me I perceive myself to be, and it is based on the world around me. I can see others' heights and position my own accordingly. It is a comparative measure. I am comparing myself to those around me.

Next comes the me that I think I should be. First I see what my physical height is, then I attach an assessment to that fact— tall, short etc.—and then the third me attaches a value to that description: good or bad, right or wrong, normal or abnormal. All kinds of judgments are possible. "Oh," I think, "I should be taller!" or "I am too short!" This value comes from society and society's expectation of what people should be like. Modern North American society has a vision of men being taller than women (even though many men are shorter than some women and many women are taller than some men). Therefore, I learned to believe that I am too short. My height becomes not just a fact, but a flaw. I should be something else if I wish to conform to societal norms and feel "normal."

The fourth image is the one that wants to be different. It has a vision of what I would be like if I were better than I am—or what I think would be better. This me wishes I were taller and has become dissatisfied with my real height—dissatisfied, then, with the real me.

Finally, there is the me that I fantasize about being. This imaginary me not only is very tall, but can cure cancer, abolish poverty, and always look good in everything he wears. That is the me that lives in a dream world.

These last four of the reflections are about self-image—how we see ourselves compared to how we really are and how we'd like to be. And they are about self-esteem—how we judge ourselves compared to other people and to our own belief about what we should be like. This is the most sensitive issue people have. Most mental health problems stem from low self-esteem and an inability to accept yourself for who you are. In fact, most people have a lower opinion of themselves than they should. That is not good. It is crucial to know what you are, not what you think you are, and try to make them the same. When all the me's are in balance, so are we.

I had a patient once who, unhappy with his weight, lost a hundred and fifty pounds. It had not been easy, and he should have been proud of this achievement. Yet when he looked in the mirror, he did not see the slim man he had become. He kept seeing the fat guy, who existed now only in his head. His self-image was out of balance with what he had accomplished. To balance things out between what he was and how he saw himself, I had him stand in front of a mirror every day and tell himself repeatedly that he was not carrying that weight anymore, that he had shed it and opened a new chapter in his life. It took a long time to make his self-image jive with his real image, but eventually he accomplished it. He said it often enough that he had to believe that it must be true. He was able to apply that lesson to other areas of his life as well, and his weight became an old issue he did not have to worry about anymore.

For this patient, it was easy to see where his self-image and his real self were not aligned. It was a physical discrepancy. For others, the difference is more subtle.

As mentioned in an earlier chapter, here in Newfoundland we have a label we apply to people: Come From Away or, more commonly, CFA. Though there is nothing wrong with being a CFA, the term implies that this place is not their home—that despite living here, they are not "real" Newfoundlanders. When I first moved here, I saw myself as a Come From Away, but I did not want to. I knew that if I was going to make my home here, I had to stop thinking of myself as a foreigner. So I trained myself to see a Newfoundlander when I looked in the mirror. Someone who is at home here. Someone who belongs. Now that is what I see and what I have become. Others might look at me, listen to me speak, and see a CFA, but that is not my problem. All that matters is what I see. I have aligned what I am and what I wish to be, and my me's are in balance.

It is very important that we know who we are. We are made up of so many things: our personality, our temperament, our intelligence, our body, our culture, our background, our way of doing things, our way of relating to each other, our family, our religion . . . How do all those things come together, and what do they make? I used to hold self-esteem workshops to help people figure out who they really are and to accept that self-knowledge.

Here are some of the techniques I taught in those self-esteem workshops:

- Engage in positive self-talk. Write down your strengths and weaknesses. Record affirmations—good things about yourself—spoken in your voice, and listen to them nightly or daily.

- Listen to your intuition, because it is a sure guide. Write down your creative ideas.

- Have a vision and set goals.

- Find a mentor whom you can trust, who sees your potential and can help you achieve your goals.

- Remember, people who buy lottery tickets see themselves as winners.

- Learn how to handle mistakes without thinking of them as proof that you are flawed.

- Learn how to handle criticism when it is constructive, and acknowledge where improvements can be made.

- Understand that not all criticism is constructive or accurate. Do not agree to accept criticism that is designed to make you feel bad about yourself and cannot lead to tangible improvement. Or, if criticism is partially valid, accept only that part.

- Probe and ask questions when criticism is vague, rather than assuming the worst.
- Above all, learn to laugh at your imperfections. Your weaknesses, as well as your strengths, make you human.

In my workshops, I would have participants make a specific list with topics across the top. They would judge themselves on a scale of one to ten (my nose is a minus two, for example) and create a picture of themselves. If it was real, they had to accept it and get over it. If it was not real, they had to overcome that mistaken self-image.

The same is true of what we fantasize about being. Perhaps someone dreams about being a world-class sprinter, but if they are not fast enough and if no amount of training will make them so, they will never be able to compete on a world stage. Instead of dwelling on it, they must focus their attention on what they can do—on what they really are. That person may not be a world champion runner. However, they may be a great swimmer. If not, perhaps they are a competent swimmer or a competent runner. In any case, to be healthy, to be in balance, they must be content with never being that champion they dream of becoming. That may be hard, but it is true.

However, the good news is that I have seen many people over the years work on their self-esteem and self-image. By accepting their limitations and their strengths, and getting rid of their self-critic, they have become champions of their own lives.

THE VALLENATO LEGENDS FESTIVAL

VALLEDUPAR HAS BEEN classified as the hottest place in Colombia. Maybe that is because of the temperature—its average high is around thirty-five degrees Celsius. But it might also be because of the Vallenato folk music that is indigenous to the region. The music, a fusion of Spanish, West African, and South American indigenous styles, is recognized as an Intangible Cultural Heritage by UNESCO.

As a Colombian, my wife Clarines is a big fan of Vallenato music. Every year, Valledupar holds a three-day Vallenato Legends Festival. Recently, to celebrate her birthday, we flew to Colombia, accompanied by our son and daughter, and attended the festival. We were joined by several members of our family who live in Colombia. It was quite a reunion.

When we arrived at the airport, we were greeted with live music, dancing, and cold Colombian beer. What a beautiful way to begin our holiday. Everything—our transportation, our accommodations, the food, the drink—was perfect. Music was everywhere and people looked both happy and busy.

I speak very little Spanish, which, in addition to my hearing problem, meant I did not understand any of the lyrics to the songs we heard, but I could feel the music. It was so dynamic and active. It reminded me of my homeland and the singing of poetry from *The Book of Kings*. The songs told the stories of the people of the region and though some of the stories were sad, the music was happy and uplifting.

I listened to the singers without understanding their words. My wife, son, daughter, and other family members, who are fluent in Spanish, sang along and danced happily.

In my eyes, as an outsider, it seemed as if the music and

dancing was in the South American blood and happiness prevailed. For five or six hours I sat with my family and listened to singing I could not understand, and I was made happy by seeing the happiness of those around me.

The festival started at seven each evening each day and ran to almost seven in the morning. At three a.m., people were still jumping up and down, watching and listening to the musicians. I was struck by how people allowed themselves to be happy and truly have a good time. They were celebrating together, and it was a joyous occasion.

The third night is the culmination of the festival and even bigger than the first two evenings. Our taxi brought us as close as it could to the large park where the concert was being held and we joined the crowd making its way to the venue. We had been warned about pickpockets and were on our guard. Unfortunately, we were not careful enough.

I was walking along when suddenly I was pushed hard from the side. As I tried to keep myself from falling, my son, who was walking behind me, reached out to grab me. No sooner had he helped me than he realized his wallet had been stolen. Obviously, the push was a ploy to distract us and grab the wallet.

It took just a few moments for happiness and joy to be replaced by confusion and stress. My son felt violated, and the mood dropped even further when another family member pointed out that they had even stolen his ticket for that night's performance.

Fortunately, no one was hurt, but such an act of violation is extremely stressful. To make matters worse, there were a couple of police officers nearby. We told them what happened, and they simply walked away, saying with a shrug, "You should not bring your wallet with you in this crowd." That was it!

Rather than carry on into the festival, we decided to go back to our residence. We could talk of little else but the robbery, what we should and should not have done, and what steps would now have to be taken, such as cancelling all my son's credit cards.

I saw the support and kindness being extended to my son and how everyone was trying their best to help and make things easier for him. I thought about how this kind of thing affects us and how I had the right to be upset about it. I decided not to go down that path. I remembered two old sayings from my homeland, "The end of night is a bright morning," and "At the heart of no hope there is plenty of hope."

But such optimistic musings are not unique to the Persian culture. In his book *Good to Great*, author Jim Collins coined the phrase "the Stockdale Paradox." Admiral James B. Stockdale spent eight years as a prisoner of war at the Hanoi Hilton, the notorious prison where American soldiers were held during the Vietnam War. Stockdale was tortured repeatedly and lived in appalling conditions. He had no reason to believe that he would survive the experience. Yet he found a way to stay alive by embracing a healthy and realistic optimism.

We must recognize and deal with our situation realistically, no matter how dire, without ever giving up on the belief that we will get through it. Taking that concept as my guide, that night I told myself we would do whatever we had to do, but we had a choice about being upset and feeling hopeless. We would not choose those feelings.

The next day, my son and another family member decided to go to the police department and document the robbery. Another family member knew the owner of the local newspaper and told him about the robbery. The owner then contacted the local governor to tell him what happened.

Meanwhile, our taxi driver contacted all the local radio stations, told them what had happened, and announced there would be a reward for the return of the wallet. In short order, the news of the robbery of a Canadian doctor spread everywhere and the response was all we could wish.

The governor's office called and spoke to my son, telling him that a top-ranking police official would be coming to discuss the matter with him. This official soon arrived and it was clear that the robbery was considered a publicity nightmare by the powers that be.

However, from our point of view, all the publicity was a good thing. Late that afternoon, one of the radio stations called and said that the wallet had been found and someone would return it to my son. When he got it back, the documents were intact, but all the money had disappeared.

When I look back on this incident, I think that we did everything right to facilitate the return of the wallet. We were upset, but never lost sight of the fact that though we could not control the situation, we could control our response to it. We lost a wallet, but we did not lose our spirit.

As a result, the entire experience was not ruined. In fact, collectively, it was a positive experience. We all worked together to make it so. Just as it sometimes happens that a place can improve after a war, flood, or some other disaster, so it was with our family. We felt we came out winners.

It would have ended up being a positive experience even if the wallet had not been returned. We began our journey happily and we ended it happily—with music and family.

FIXING BLAME

IS THERE ANYTHING more commonplace than blame? When something goes wrong, we always seem to point a finger. We find a reason for what happened. We try to fix the blame. Does this sound familiar?

I was late for work because . . .

- the traffic was bad
- other drivers are idiots
- my alarm did not go off

I drank too much last night because . . .

- my job is terrible and my boss is unreasonable
- my friends were all drinking a lot
- my girlfriend broke up with me

I am overweight because . . .

- my mother's such a good cook
- advertisers con me into buying high-calorie products
- restaurants serve portions that are too big
- I do not have time to exercise

We blame someone else. The other drivers should have taken more care; our boss should not have been so mean; restaurants should not load up our plates. It's not us, it's them. So we don't have to do anything about it, and we feel perfectly justified in this. As if by fixing the blame, we have somehow solved a problem.

Sometimes we even blame ourselves. We think, "I did not get that job because I blew the interview. I am so stupid!" And we cannot stop thinking about it—but we are not moving towards a solution, because there is no solution.

What we need to realize is that we have not solved anything by placing blame. Blame is a dysfunctional coping mechanism. We justify our own feelings by assigning blame. We think, "They should have done this or that." And because others did not act as we believe they should have, we somehow feel we are no longer responsible for the outcome—we are just victims of circumstances and of other people. Case closed.

Sometimes, this may be the case. Sometimes we are helpless victims of others' bad behaviour. Whatever bad thing has happened, it is all someone else's fault. We have a right to be furious. But where does that anger get us? Is it worth the time and energy it takes away from our pursuit of a good life?

I once had a patient who worked in human resources for a large corporation. The company was restructuring, and it was his job to hand out the pink slips. He was extremely careful to explain to people why they were being let go and felt perfectly justified in the job he was doing. I saw quite a few of the people who had been laid off in my practice, and they all complained and blamed the company—something he did not do.

Then came the day when almost all the pink slips had been handed out, when almost all the people who were going to be let go had been let go. There was only one more person to fire. The last one to receive a pink slip was the man who had handed out so many to others. With no one left to fire, the company had no reason to keep him. Did he accept this and move on? No! He was furious. He blamed the company for firing him after he had done all the dirty work and felt completely justified being upset.

However, blame is all inside our mind. Fixing the blame will not change anything. It will not ease the traffic. It will not make the alarm clock ring. It will not bring your girlfriend back. So there is no point to it, and the way to correct it is to get over it. Do not dwell on what should have happened, on who should have acted differently. Accept it and understand it. If necessary, get as miserable as you like, but only for a short period. Then stop. Move on.

A little while ago, I was in a grocery store parking lot, and three men came up to me and started yelling, accusing me of all kinds of driving faults and just generally trying to pick a fight. It was very upsetting. They were a lot younger than me, and I was in no position to fight them off if they attacked. Although there were other people around, the bystanders did nothing to help, not even the two employees who were watching what was happening. I was on my own, and I had nowhere to turn for help. What could I do? There was only one answer. By remaining calm, I was slowly able to defuse the situation and eventually the bullies left, squealing their tires, still cursing at me. I went into the store to talk to the manager, but he could not help. I went home and phoned the police. I was able to give them part of the licence plate number, but without video surveillance, which the store did not have, they did not think there was much they could do.

What could I do? I sat down that evening and thought about it. Well, the first thing I could do was fix the blame. Why did this happen to me? I came up with several possible answers. They picked on me because of my race. They picked on me because the world is going to hell. I could even blame myself—I must have done something to provoke them. Then I broadened the accusations. The people around should have helped. The manager should have done something. The police should have caught them. Because. Because. Because. Should. Should. Should.

The only thing that fixing the blame would do was make me even more upset. I had to get up and go to work the next morning whether I had slept all night or tossed and turned and railed against the world. What good would that do me?

I decided I would move on. I would not be held in one place, fixating on one situation. I would not be a victim. Even though I had the "right" to be upset, it did not mean that I should be. I had done what I could. I had taken all the logical steps to address the situation. Continuing to dwell on what happened would just be punishing myself, and that is the only thing I am in complete control of. So I chose to let it go. I went to bed and was well-rested the next morning.

Had I fixed the blame? No. I had recognized that fixing the blame did not fix anything.

MAKING FRIENDS WITH TIME

TIME IS A valuable commodity that should not be wasted.

But how often do we see time as our enemy? When we are in our working years, we do not seem to have enough of it. We work too much. We have too many personal and family obligations. We have all kinds of things demanding our time. Time becomes our enemy because we have too much to do and not enough time to do it in. Later in life, when we are not working, when we are retired or when we simply do not have a schedule of activities, we have too much time and nothing to do with it, so time becomes our enemy again.

Is time really our enemy? Most of us never consider that question. I think we need to accept time as our friend. Because it is finite. We have less of it every day until it is finally all gone. I remind myself of this by going to the cemetery. It may sound morbid, but it is not. I stand facing a gravestone and every time I go, I stand a little closer. This is to show myself that I have less time remaining. It reminds me to use my time wisely and to enjoy spending it.

Most of us have a limited amount of money, but we do not see money as an enemy. When you have a hundred dollars to spend, you feel good. Your imagination starts to work. You think, "I can buy those shoes I saw at the mall," or "I can go out for dinner at that new restaurant." We must learn to see time the same way and treat it as a gift.

Of course, just as you spend money on necessities as well as on indulgences, you must also spend time doing a lot of things that are obligations rather than pleasures. However, as with money, you should never give so much of it away that you have nothing left for yourself, and you should spend it wisely.

So many people talk about how they work Monday to Friday just to make it to the weekend when they can enjoy themselves. This makes me sad. We should not spend all that time without enjoying it. Yes, we must work, but we need to find ways to enjoy that time as well as the time we are not working.

Look at how we spend our money. We need to spend money on shelter—we have no choice—and we might not like the place we live. It might be too small; it might be in the wrong neighbourhood. The people next door might be unpleasant. Yet we still fix it up and make it as nice as we can. We can do the same with time when we must spend it somewhere we would rather not be. For example, we can give ourselves little gifts of time in the form of good memories. Stop to remember something nice when things are looking glum, just as you would stop to have a drink of water if you were thirsty. It is a bit of relief from an unpleasant situation, just as a drink is a bit of relief from thirst. Our brain can be trained to dwell on good things, just as it can be trained to dwell on bad things. We must teach it. Decorate our mind the way we decorate our living space.

So do not just trudge to the car or to the bus, head down and shoulders hunched. Look at the flowers. Watch the people around you. Since you must take that walk regardless, teach yourself to enjoy the time you spend doing it.

Do not leave time unused. If you go for a cup of coffee that costs three dollars and you hand over five, you wait for your change. You may choose to give it as a tip to the person who served you, you may choose to put it in a charity jar on the counter, or you may choose to put it back in your wallet. But you do not just leave it lying there. You decide how it will be spent. Yet we are all guilty of leaving much too much time on the counter because we have chosen not to do something with it.

A few days ago, I found myself locked out of my car. How frustrating. There was nothing I could do other than call my daughter and ask her if she could bring me a spare key. She agreed, but I had to wait about twenty minutes for her to arrive. I could have railed against the circumstances that left me hanging around and complained to myself about how much time I was wasting when there was so much else I could be doing, but I did not. Instead, I used that time to walk around a new neighbourhood and enjoy being outdoors. I did not leave my time lying on the counter unspent. I did not waste it feeling bad—I treated it as a gift. Things happen. Make the best of it.

I have seen people pick at themselves physically or pick at others by criticizing and gossiping just to fill time. Some people go so far as to make up stories and interfere with other people's business for the same reason. They are spending their time very badly, turning sour and mean what could be sweet.

Complaints about not having enough time are common. That is why it is ironic how often people spend time doing things that are not necessary. They acquire obligations and then just continue with them. Maybe it is attending a church, mosque, or temple they no longer believe in. Maybe it is playing a sport they no longer enjoy. Maybe it is routinely having lunch with an old friend they no longer care about. We need to study our time every so often and measure the value of the things we spend it on. Then we must stop doing the things that have become obligations without merit.

I had one patient who came to see me once or twice a year. In her nineties, she was always truly clear on why she was there. She understood that we do not get a do-over when it comes to the commodity of time. Once it is gone, it is gone. We need to limit the number of times we say to ourselves, "If I had my time back, this is what I would do differently."

This older woman always had five or six things she wanted me to plan out with her for the next six months, like what to do with her husband, with her bridge club, and so on. I used to say that she came in for a tune-up and oil change, to make sure she kept running smoothly. It was always a pleasure to see her.

In fact, it is these kinds of interactions that make me love my profession so much. I am not perfect, and because I love my profession, sometimes I am guilty of overspending time on this aspect of my life—kind of like deciding to go out for two beers and always staying for four.

We need to make peace with time. That means understanding how much we have and deciding how we are going to spend it. Only then will we be able to have fun with time.

POLE! POLE!

WHEN I WAS growing up, I loved watching old black and white movies. I remember one in particular—*The Snows of Kilimanjaro*, starring Gregory Peck and Susan Hayward and based on an Ernest Hemingway short story. What drew me was not the story itself: it was Mount Kilimanjaro and the jungles of Africa, alive with elephants and lions.

I saw other movies and documentaries, and in my thoughts I was actually there, travelling side by side with the people on the screen through the heat of the jungle and the snows of Africa's highest mountain. It is because of all those films I watched over the years that travelling to the jungles of Africa and climbing Mount Kilimanjaro became one of the entries on my bucket list.

After the four-day hike in Machu Picchu in 2007 and the four-day hike in the Long-Range Mountains of Newfoundland, I decided the time had come to climb Mount Kilimanjaro. The climb was also on my hiking buddy Pat's bucket list, so he was the obvious person to approach about getting such a venture in motion. Fortunately, Pat is more organized than me and he took the lead, doing the research on when and how to make the climb. Johnny was eager to join us. I also approached John, who was both my friend and my family doctor. We held a meeting and decided that the trip was on.

Now it was time to prepare. I went online to learn everything I needed to know and had to do. Mount Kilimanjaro is in Tanzania, East Africa. At 5,895 metres (19,340 feet) above sea level, it is the highest mountain in Africa. In January, when we would be going, the temperature at the base of the mountain averages thirty degrees Celsius, but at the summit that number drops to minus twenty. That is the difference between a day at the beach under the broiling sun and the inside of a medical-grade freezer, but that is not really the problem. The problem is that the atmospheric pressure drops by about a tenth for every thousand metres increase in altitude. So, at the top of Mount Kilimanjaro, the air pressure is only about forty per cent of that found at sea level. That is enough to manage on, but it makes it a lot more difficult to fill the lungs; altitude sickness becomes a real danger.

One of the websites I visited said a person who could run ten kilometres in sixty-five minutes without a problem would be fit enough to climb the mountain. I could easily run that distance in fifty-five minutes, even at the age of sixty-two, which was how old I was when we were preparing for the climb. I exercised daily to keep in shape. I was determined to scratch this childhood dream off my bucket list.

However, there was a problem. Years ago, after many tests, I was diagnosed with thalassemia minor, a condition that causes a slight lowering of the hemoglobin levels in my blood and smaller red blood cells than the norm. It is a genetic disorder mostly found in people from the Mediterranean area. I have lived with it for a long time.

One day, a couple of months before our trip, John came into my office after hours and told me, "You cannot go." The people in the hematology department had told him to tell me that at high altitudes my body could break down and I could die. John was a very experienced and competent doctor, and I fully understood and did not doubt what he was saying. Nonetheless, I balked. "I know me, and I am very familiar with the mind and body connection," I told him. "If my body tells me to stop, I will go no farther."

The issue of a mind and body connection is well-documented

in health literature. Listening to the body's message is important. For example, your body is aching, and both your body and mind are sluggish. You feel exhausted. Whether or not it is your usual bedtime, your body is asking for rest, and you should heed that call if you possibly can.

John reluctantly agreed, but I knew my health was on his mind. We decided I would take a blood test before we went and, if I came back, repeat it to see what impact the trip had had on my condition.

At the same time this was going on, I was also discovering many interesting facts about the place we were headed. For example, Tanzania produces a purple-blue gemstone called tanzanite, which is worth about five to six hundred dollars per carat. I also discovered that Zanzibar is part of Tanzania. The island has an interesting connection to my homeland. The story goes that many years ago there was a Khan from the city of Shiraz in the south of Iran who was paranoid and believed that he had enemies determined to kill his family and followers. So he loaded hundreds of people on a ship and moved to Zanzibar. The Persian language and culture (including the celebration of our new year, Norouz) mixed with the local Swahili traditions and culture to the extent that when I visited, I could understand many words spoken there, despite the generations that had passed since the Khan's arrival.

Our trip eventually began and before long the four of us were in Arusha, the small Tanzanian city from which we would set out on our adventure. The next day, a Land Rover with a raised ceiling picked us up for our four-day Serengeti jungle safari. The beauty of nature in this jungle is shown over and over in movies, but it is more beautiful, especially when you see the indigenous Maasai people in their own homes in the jungle.

The day finally arrived when we found ourselves at the foot of Mount Kilimanjaro. Before we began our climb, we met up with a married couple who would be joining us. That made for a total of six hikers, as well as the twenty-seven local men who would guide and manage the trip.

The first thing I heard from the guide, and maybe the most memorable, was *Pole, pole*, pronounced poley, poley, which was Swahili for "slowly, slowly." I took this advice to heart and went up the mountain *pole, pole*. I think this was particularly important because it allowed my body to acclimatize gradually to the decreasing atmospheric pressure. I listened to my body very carefully and it did not tell me to stop. For seven days as we climbed all the way up, *pole, pole* was my mantra.

On the seventh day, we arrived at Stella Point, located on the southern crater rim of Kibo, the tallest of Kilimanjaro's three peaks. This is the arctic zone of the mountain, a region with no rainfall, high winds, and sub-zero temperatures. There were no plants, no animals, and no insects. At this point, the toughest part of the route is over. We were about sixty minutes from Uhuru Point, which is the summit, and had to cross the seven slopes of Kibo and climb a ridge to get there.

At that point, the wisdom of my continuation to the summit had to be discussed, not only by the two doctors on the trip, Pat and John, but also by the guides, who knew best what we were facing. We had brought a portable pulse oximeter with us to monitor our oxygen saturation. It is a little clamp you put on your fingertip and it shows how much oxygen you have in your blood. Normal pulse oxygen levels, which is what this machine reads, range from ninety-five to one hundred per cent. Values under sixty per cent are dangerous. All our numbers were dropping as we climbed, but one night my reading was below sixty. Pat and John were aware of this and watched over me.

After talking it over, they decided to allow me to continue, and at about 3 p.m. we arrived at the top of Mount Kilimanjaro. I know I cried as I arrived. I had waited for this moment for so long. We managed to call our families with special phones we had rented at home, so I was able to share that moment with them. It was the first time I had ever stood above the clouds—what an exciting moment! We hugged and laughed and took pictures.

After about half an hour, we started to climb down into the crater formed by the extinct volcano. We only went about 250 feet inside because breathing was very rough, and we had to be extremely careful not to exert too much pressure on our bodies. I had to move very gently, and I had very little appetite because of the toll the trip at such a high altitude was taking on me. But it was beautiful inside the crater with the snow and the glaciers around. We slept there that night and arose the next morning for our trip back down the mountain. It took us two days to travel the sixty-two kilometres back.

I will always treasure the memory of that hike to the top of Mount Kilimanjaro. Not just for the scenery, but the experience of believing in myself and depending on the friendship of my hiking buddies. It is something I will always remember. I recall every day of that hike and still hear our young guide telling us *Pole, pole*.

In our everyday lives we need to be more patient and use *pole, pole* to reach our goals. We need to hold on to a picture of our life and see all the good things in it. Too often, society teaches us to hang on to the memories of the bad events. I say no. Hang on to the good memories. After nine years, the hike up Mount

Kilimanjaro is still alive and well in my mind. It always will be.

On that trip, I learned so much about life and about the connections between people, and there was a physical benefit as well. When I returned, I had the blood test performed, as promised, and the results were astonishing. My thalassemia had improved, and, instead of worsening, my red blood cell count had increased. Rather than killing me, my climb had improved my health. What a blessing.

MOTHER MAY I?

THERE IS AN old children's game called "Mother, May I?" in which a bunch of players stand in a line and ask permission to move closer and closer to the player designated "Mother," who stands at the other end of the room with her back turned towards the rest of the players. The person who reaches Mother first gets to be Mother next time. The most important rule is that no one gets to move without first asking "Mother, May I?" Whether she says yes or no, the player must abide by that decision.

Sometimes, I think we all get stuck playing "Mother, May I?" even when we become adults. I do not mean that we still ask our mothers before we do anything. I mean that we do not give ourselves permission to act.

A few years ago, I was visiting a park in the United States with a friend of mine. He wanted to smoke a cigar. No one else around was smoking, but there were no signs saying it was against the rules. Nonetheless, I suggested we ask a park employee if it was allowed. The person we spoke to was thunderstruck.

"No! You should not smoke here!" he cried.

Did he even know this for sure? I think he was stuck in his own childhood, unable to move on from all the restrictions that were drilled into him as a child. (Of course, we felt the need to ask permission before behaving in a certain way, so we are not immune either.) And if you carry around an internal belief in a lot of restrictions, then you will continue to impose restrictions on yourself.

Restrictions are not always a bad thing. A few chapters ago, I wrote about a man who lived next to the airport. It was very noisy, but the sound of the planes landing and taking off did not bother him at all. That is because he did not give his brain permission to process the noise.

However, too often we give ourselves permission to respond in a negative way to our situation and, perhaps, to over-respond. Everyone has negative emotions. We all get angry or hurt or ashamed. That is natural. However, we will stay in that negative state if we let ourselves. We stay angry far longer than the situation warrants, and that is not healthy.

Other times, we do the opposite. We do not give ourselves permission. We spend our lives not allowing ourselves to do something we would like to do—or perhaps not even learning what it is we would like to do. We do this because somehow, somewhere we have become afraid. So we send negative messages to ourselves. We say, "I am not good enough, I am not smart enough, I am not attractive enough, I am not brave enough," or we put ourselves down with direct internal orders: "You cannot do this!" or "You must not even think about doing that!"

Think about shy people. They do not permit themselves to come out of their shell. They do not permit themselves to let go of past mistakes, past hurts, or past anger. So they do not fully live in the present.

The past can be immensely powerful, and it can restrict the present. You may have done something when you were young that coloured your life. Perhaps you lied, or shoplifted, or maybe you just ate too many cookies. But you learned your lesson and did not do it again. However, instead of letting go, many people never permit themselves to wash those negative memories we talked about in a previous chapter from their brain.

No wonder! Our parents, our schools, our whole society was right there telling us how bad we were when we made that mistake. So we do not forgive ourselves.

We need to challenge our belief that things are the way they are because of factors beyond our control. Just yesterday, a young woman came to see me. She was talking to me and crying. Although the issue we were discussing was important, there was no need to cry over it. So, I asked her, quite politely, why she was crying. She answered simply, "That's me. I cry easily." I asked her again where this notion came from and she just said, "I don't know."

She had given herself permission to cry, whether there was a reason for it or not. Rather than repressing the urge to cry, she had allowed her mind and body to act as if she had given permission for the tears to flow. Now, crying came "easily," as she said, without a logical reason.

Challenging our beliefs will make us think twice about what we take for granted. We say things to ourselves so often and over such a long period of time that we end up believing them. Whether it is the belief that we are a bad person because we broke a law thirty years ago or the belief that we cry easily, we should question these assumptions. If we study what things we permit ourselves to do, we can stop validating the ones that are nonsense.

THE POWER OF "SHOULD"

IF THERE IS one word in the English language that has a true superpower, it is "should." It's an immensely powerful word. It tells you that if you do not act, behave, or think in a certain way, you are doing things wrong.

And no one wants to do things wrong.

We use the word all the time. Lying in bed first thing in the morning, comfortable and still sleepy, we think: *I should get up.* If we do not get up, we feel guilty. We believe that just by lying in bed we are doing something wrong, and that is only the beginning—a simple example. Our entire day—our entire life—is full of things we should do, should become, or should be. Should think. Should believe. Should. Should. Should.

I am the youngest member of my family. When I was growing up in a traditional Iranian household, my mother used to tell me that because of my birth position, it was my duty to take care of her. Everyone in the family—all my siblings—believed this to be true. When I left to go to school in the United States, she told me I was supposed to come back home to fulfill that obligation, but I did not. I stayed in North America and followed my own path, not the one laid out for me by the expectations of my mother and the rest of my family. The result was that for years I felt guilty and depressed because I had not done what I *should* have done. There was an imbalance between the real "me" and the 'me' that everyone (including myself, because part of me did want to return home and take care of her) thought I should have been. I was letting "should" make my life miserable.

We must remember that it is not about right or wrong. There are many ways of doing things. The belief of my family that I should take care of our mother was based solely on tradition.

Others could (and did) care for her just as well or better. The same would have been true had she gone into a seniors' home, as is more common in North America. Our countries just have different traditions—traditions that have hardened into a belief about the way things should or should not be done. That does not mean one nationality loves their elders more than the other, or that one nationality treats their elders better than the other. It just means they have taken different paths.

Of course, we need the word "should." It encapsulates our relationship with the world around us. It is how we learn about society's expectations, about our culture, about our religion, about our place in all that, but we need to keep it in check. Other people's beliefs about how we should run our lives should not run our lives.

We are not born free into a world that allows us to do anything we want. Our first introduction to "should" comes almost as soon as we are born. To a small baby, the entire outside world is represented by its parents. The baby has itself, its own wants and needs, and it has its parents, who provide everything they think the child should have—not just food, warmth, and other necessities, but, as the child grows, morals, culture, religion, and all the intangibles that go into making our lives well-rounded and turning us into people who can function in society.

These two forces start out equal in the child. Think of a circle divided in half. If these two forces were colours, the child's half of the circle would be yellow and the parent's half would be blue, and they would exist side by side. Eventually, however, the child grows up and naturally begins to question its parents and make its own observations about the world. At this point, a third colour enters the picture. It is neither yellow nor blue but green—a strip of colour between the two others that combines them into one. This is the colour of the child learning to make its own decisions. This is the colour of the child becoming an individual, an adult. Gradually, the green strip should grow wider and wider until the sphere of childhood—all about what it wants—and the world of parental and societal "should" are pushed to the peripheries. Of course, both of those things are still important. However, they are in balance working together to make a pleasing green—a combination of what we want and what society expects of us.

But sometimes we let "should" overcome us and our circle starts to turn too blue. So many people have expectations of how the world—their world—should work: they should get this kind of job, they should be married by thirty, they should have a house by thirty-five, and so on. If they have accomplished all those things, they find other criteria to show that they have somehow failed: they should have a better job, they should have a closer marriage, they should have a bigger house. They allow themselves to be ruled by the things they have been taught they should be.

This happens at every level of our lives. I see many couples who have allowed their beliefs about how things should be done interfere with their relationship, and there is no right or wrong involved.

I once had a couple come to see me who fought all the time because they had different ways of doing things. The husband got home from work earlier than the wife. He used this half-hour to sit back and relax after his busy day. When the wife got home, she would be furious because he had not tidied up or started cooking dinner or completed a number of other tasks that she felt "should" be done before one allowed oneself to sit down.

The husband was more than willing to share the household

tasks—he just didn't want to tackle them on her prescribed schedule. This caused a great deal of strain in their marriage. Neither one was right. Neither one was wrong. However, they were both being ruled by how things "should" be done, and the wife needed to let go of those expectations. She was confusing what really should be and the way she wanted things to be. She had to learn to stop judging her husband for doing things differently from the way she preferred, which she had translated into the way things "should" be done.

There is one relationship even closer than that between spouses. That is the relationship we have with ourselves—the person we are with 24/7, 365 days a year. We need to find the balance between what we want and what we think we should have. Between the me we really are and the me we think we should be.

IQ, EQ, SQ, WE ALL QUEUE

HAVE YOU EVER walked into a store absolutely determined that you are just looking and then, half an hour later, walked out with a completely spur-of-the-moment purchase? I think we all have. You did not mean to buy anything, but somehow the salesperson made it sound like such a good idea that you feel foolish not buying it. What does that salesperson have that makes them so good at influencing others' decisions?

There are several kinds of intelligence. We are probably most familiar with the concept of measuring people's IQ, or intelligence quotient. That is how brainy someone is and counts people with a lot of book learning—the kind of people who either know the answer or can figure it out.

Then there are people with EQ (emotional quotient), or

emotional intelligence. They can recognize their own emotions and the emotions of others and use that knowledge to guide their actions. They are often labelled as having common sense.

Those wizard salespeople? They have SQ (social quotient), or social intelligence. Some people call their ability "street smarts," and it seems that people with social intelligence are more successful and healthier than the rest of us.

We know that social intelligence and emotional intelligence are connected, but what exactly is social intelligence, and how is it connected to other intelligences?

Social intelligence is the ability to successfully build relationships and navigate social environments. According to Dr. Daniel Goleman in his book *Social Intelligence: The New Science of Human Relationships*,[8] our brains are built to optimize relationships. He identifies two aspects of protoconversation, which is a kind of subtext of gestures and intonation:

1. **Social Awareness:** Sensing other people's feelings with full receptivity and empathetic accuracy, using and understanding the social world and relationships web.

2. **Social Facility:** Interacting smoothly, knowing how you come across, and being able to improve the outcome of social interactors and caring for their needs.

Dr. Goleman talks about the "low road," the emotional-based way we process interactions. "It's how we read body-language, facial expressions and then formulate gut feelings about people." We also have a "high road," the part of us that uses logical critical

[8] Goleman, D. (2006). *Social Intelligence: The New Science of Human Relationships.* New York: Bantam Books.

thinking. We use the high road to communicate, tell stories, and make connections.

He goes on to explain that past negative experiences cause our low roads to give us social anxiety. He calls it social triggering, and we need to be aware of these social triggers and work to get through them.

Normally, people with emotional intelligence know their low road and can put their high road to good use. This happens to me every day. When a patient becomes emotional, whether negative or positive, I sense that and I feel it in my gut (low road), but I use my experience and skill (high road) to interact with them.

We want to be comfortable in social situations where there are other people and good in our interactions, so we need to exercise our social intelligence.

Dr. Ronald Riggio, the author of the blog *Cutting-Edge Leadership*, claims that social intelligence is the key to career and life success.[9] In the article, Dr. Riggio explains the following six elements of social intelligence:

1. Having social expressiveness skills, particularly good verbal fluency and conversation skills—I think this starts at home. We need to teach our young people to exercise good conversation skills, rather than allowing them to spend all their time on their phones or other electronic devices.

2. Knowing the social rules, knowing how to play the game of social interaction—People stand in grocery lines and bus lines; they sit in waiting rooms. They

[9] Riggio, Ronald E. "What is social intelligence? Why does it matter?" July 1, 2014. Online at https://www.psychologytoday.com/ca/blog/cutting-edge-leadership/201407/what-is-social-intelligence-why-does-it-matter.

need to know how to act towards one another in these situations and how to carry on a conversation.

3. Understanding how to be a genuinely good listener—When you talk to a person with high social intelligence, you feel you have a good connection with him or her. I once read about the late Dr. Wallace Ingram, who told his medical students that if they listened to patients, those patients would provide the diagnosis and treatment plan. I find this to be true with my patients as well.

4. "Understanding what makes other people tick"— Using our emotional intelligence to attune ourselves to what others say and how they are behaving. It takes practice and persistence to develop this aspect of social and emotional intelligence.

5. Being able to play different social roles and to have the confidence to engage in social interactional talking to initiate and maintain interpersonal relationships—Examples of this include how well you express your opinion, how well you chat with an unfamiliar person, and how well you can tell someone they are doing something you do not like.

6. Having impression management skills—This is showing others your true self or the image you want them to perceive. In my practice, my patients need to see me as a confident doctor, but they also need to see me as I really am. For example, I try to dress well at work and show respect for all the social rules, but when I am listening and expressing myself, I am

honest and genuine. If, as Dr. Riggio explains, "we fall into the dangerous art of impression management," then we must be really good at it. I am not personally engaged in this game.

We can improve our social intelligence by learning more about ourselves. In *Social Intelligence*, Dr. Goleman suggests that when you have social triggers, you should ask yourself the following questions:

> › What kind of social interaction do I dread?
> › Who do I feel anxious hanging out with?
> › When do I feel I cannot be myself?

I think this is a good start to learning the skills necessary to overcome discomfort. It is doable. But we are not computers. Sometimes we just lose it. If we listen to our bodies, we can tell when that is about to happen and stop it.

For example, if I start to get angry, I can tell because my mouth gets dry; if I am hurt, I feel like I am falling; and if I am scared my body shrinks back and my head pulls in like a turtle's. When any of these physical things happen, I know that something has triggered my low road and that it is time to activate my high-road skills. I tell myself I am a doctor, not a child, and I have the skills to overcome this.

It can help to pull back and try to pretend you are watching what is happening, rather than participating in it. I call this the "movie theatre exercise." I imagine that I am in a theatre watching a movie about what is happening to me. To take the high road, I place myself in the director's chair and change what is happening in the scene. As the director, I am the one in control.

Social intelligence and having empathy are important for health and success, and they might even come in handy for dealing with smooth salespeople!

NOW HEAR THIS!

O N A WEBSITE called *Kiss This Guy*, people post the lyrics they thought they heard rather than the actual words to a song. It's funny to read some of the things people believed singers were singing, and it is not uncommon. Just about everyone can recall at least one song they have misheard . . . but then there is me.

I never know what a singer is saying until I see the lyrics written down. It's not an occasional amusing misinterpretation: it's my reality. When other people are asking to have the volume turned down, I am asking to have the volume turned up.

You see, I have a hearing impairment. I've had it my entire life, so I am intimately acquainted with what that means. For one thing, it means that people like me must figure it out for ourselves because we are not actually deaf, and we do not have a special language or a special school to teach us how to function with diminished hearing. And that is pretty much what I have done.

People with normal hearing, or people who have never lived with someone with impaired hearing, do not really know what it's like. They take their hearing for granted. So I thought I would explain what my life is like as a person with a hearing problem functioning in the modern world. The following are just a matter of routine for me: I must ask the person next to me at the airport or in some other public space what the announcement was because I cannot understand the speaker. I am often left out of the conversation, even when it's about something I am passionately interested in, because I cannot follow what everyone is saying. Other people get frustrated with me because I cannot hear them properly. I am always asking people to speak up.

In a class or at a presentation, I always have to sit in the front. I have to give 100 per cent of my attention. I can never really trust what I heard in case I didn't hear it correctly. I get frustrated because I look stupid when there is a conversation going on around me. And I cannot fully appreciate music and poetry being read aloud because I cannot hear them completely. I frequently get numbers, emails, and addresses wrong if they are told to me over the phone.

I have a problem saying certain words and sounds because I cannot hear them properly. Being hard of hearing has had a big impact on my speech development.

People are resilient and do what they must do. Sometimes, having a hearing problem can be funny. I remember when I lived in Kansas, I was chatting with my neighbour, and he told me he was "out working in his shit." I did not think twice about it because I had heard the same thing from other people as well. I only used to wonder how such an odd expression came to be. *Why do they call that outbuilding a shit?* I used to ask myself. Then one day I understood what my neighbour was saying. He was working in his *shed*. That made a lot more sense—and was probably a lot cleaner too!

However, at other times it is not so amusing. About thirty years ago, the CBC asked me to appear on one of their shows to provide commentary on the possible psychological effects of a strike on members of a union. I was quite happy to agree and went down to the studio the next morning. We had what I thought was a great interview, and I was looking forward to seeing the broadcast the next day.

However, later that day the producer called and told me that they would not be running the interview. While the content was excellent, she said, my speech problem (not my accent—that was okay) meant they could not use the tape. I must admit that hurt, but I got what she meant.

This is when I decided I had to do something about my problem, and I had a speech assessment done. The speech pathologist was superb. She told me that because I did not hear well, my speech had not been developed properly. She told me that the volume I spoke at was low and the timbre of my voice was high. They needed to be reversed. In addition, certain English sounds like "s" and "th" and "v" and "w" were not properly developed. Instead of "thinking," I'd say "sinking," and instead of "very well" I'd say "wery well." Suddenly, a lot of things made sense.

As a result, I finally got some hearing aids. Boy, oh boy! What a huge difference it made. After that, I was able to work much better and participate in groups and conferences. I can even choose what I want to hear, so I do not wear them in certain noisy places where I'm liable to hear things I do not want to hear. (I probably should not admit to that. My audiologist, Dr. Erin Squarey, says, "We generally recommend wearing hearing aids during all waking hours to help the brain establish a new normal, even in noisy environments." She is right, of course.)

Occasionally, I will see a patient who is in the same situation I was in all those years ago. Dr. Squarey explained to me that people often mistakenly equate hearing loss with vision loss. When you cannot see the newspaper or read road signs, you get an eye test and a pair of glasses, and your vision is corrected to normal. Hearing loss is harder to track, and hearing aids cannot correct your hearing to normal.

By the time someone with a hearing impairment comes to see me, they have developed a lot of anger towards other people. They have also developed low self-esteem and low confidence in social situations. They feel helpless, not knowing what to do. Hearing aids are an important part of the solution, but even with hearing aids, we still experience problems. They are not a cure-all.

A few years ago, a retired civil servant who had reached a very senior position came to see me. He was suffering from anxiety and stress because of his hearing loss. He was losing touch with his family, his friends, and his social structure. Sharing my own experiences was remarkably effective in helping him understand that he was not alone. There are many of us in the same boat.

Now he has fun with it, telling people they are whispering no matter how loudly they speak. He has given up being upset and looks to have fun with his problem.

It takes time to get to that point. There are two necessary steps to alleviate the difficulties inherent in dealing with a hearing problem. First, we need to educate ourselves, understand our situation, and get the correct device to help us hear as well as we can. Second, we need to tell others right from the beginning that we have a hearing problem and that while we do not want them to shout at us, we do need them to speak slowly, clearly, and directly to us. Most people—though sadly not all—are good with this and helpful.

A hearing problem is something that can be dealt with. We might hear "shit" instead of "shed" and say "wery well" instead of "very well," but we can live with that as long as we remember that we are not at fault and should not blame ourselves or other people because of it. That is what I "sink."

GOING GENTLY INTO THAT GOOD NIGHT

S EVERAL YEARS AGO, my friend Johnny and I walked the
Camino de Santiago in Spain. It was a long journey—
hundreds of kilometres on foot—during which I lost twenty
pounds and gained a long grey beard.

Johnny is considerably taller than I am, which means he has
a longer stride, so he tended to get ahead of me during the day.
He would leave a marker to let me know where he was if he
strayed from the path, or when he had stopped for the day. In this
way, we were able to meet up without a problem.

Well, that was the way it was supposed to happen. One day,
I missed a marker and got lost in the woods. Suddenly, the path
seemed deserted. No pilgrims in front of me. No pilgrims behind.

I could die here, I thought. *I could drop dead from a heart attack,
and no one would know, and no one would help me.* Then I asked
myself, Are you okay with that?

I realized that I was. I felt no anxiety. I was a man in his sixties
with a good profession, a loving wife and children, a happy home,
friends, and a lifetime of interesting experiences. I had nothing to
regret. If this was the end, then so be it.

Forty minutes later, I came upon a road and shortly thereafter
was reunited with John.

The realization that I could die and that I was not afraid stuck
with me. Because most of us are afraid of death. We are afraid
of our own death, and we are afraid of the death of others. The
fear of death is an anxiety that is at the root of many, many other
anxieties.

But if there is one thing in life that is certain, it is that we are
all going to die. To spend our life living in fear of that fact is to
waste what time we do have, and that is no way to live. So how

do we overcome that fear?

I believe there are three stages to dying. In reverse order they are after-death, death, and pre-death, or living. Then there are two parts to the fear of death. The first is the fear of actually dying—the drawing of our last breath as we transition from one state of being to another. The second is the fear of what comes next. What happens to us after we die?

It is while we are living that we must deal with these fears.

How do we deal with the fear of dying? First, we much realize that it is living that causes pain, not dying. When we die, we are no longer in pain. We will take our last breath and then we will stop. It is like falling asleep. We do not know when we fall asleep. We do not know which breath is the one that marks the division between our waking world and our sleeping one. Dying is the same. There is nothing about dying itself that should make us afraid. We will not even know when it is happening, even if we know it is going to happen very soon.

That leaves the fear of what happens to us after we die, and that is something we do not know, no matter who we are. The greatest philosophers, the greatest poets, the greatest religious leaders are all in the same boat. They do not know what happens after we die. They only believe what they think to be true. We can also form a belief about what happens after we die, or we can follow the beliefs of others as we were taught. It is up to us.

There is great comfort in holding a firm belief in what happens to us after we die. However, while this helps us to get through our lives without constantly worrying about what happens afterwards, we cannot know for sure. Perhaps the most import thing is to live our life, the only thing we are sure of, as well as we can.

Developmental psychologist Erik Erikson developed a theory about the eight stages of life that people go through. He said that in the eighth and final stage, we ask ourselves the question, "Is it okay to have been me?" We look at our accomplishments and decide whether our life has been happy and productive. We can be content with what we see, or we can despair.

I once had a patient whose treatment had ended; she phoned the clinic and insisted that she had to see me. I told her to come in at 6 p.m., after my last scheduled patient of the day. She arrived, terribly upset, accompanied by her husband, and I ushered them into my office. It was there she told me that she had just received a diagnosis of stage four lung cancer. She had been given a death sentence. Her oncologist had not been tactful when he told her, making it worse, but that was not why she wanted to see me. She had come to me, as a trusted authority figure, to tell her what she should do with the rest of her life. I could see the desperation in her eyes. Things had been going well. With my help, she had learned to cope with the death of her beloved twin brother the year before. And now this. I had to overcome my own sadness to help her.

I told her to stay away from the past and the future. They no longer mattered. She had to stay in the present and live it, doing the best she could every single day.

She knew what was important to her, and she concentrated on having the best life possible. As it worked out, she had another twenty-one months to live, and I saw her just two months before she died. At that meeting she told me, "The last nineteen months have been the best of my life." She died content with what she had accomplished. She was forty-nine years old.

During those last months, she took a picture of a begonia,

which she framed and gave to me because we shared a love of nature. I look at it often and think of her.

We are all going to die. We are all going to go through the experience of drawing our last breath, and we are all going to be dead afterwards. If we can live our lives in a meaningful way and are able to look back on accomplishments we are proud of, we can overcome our fear of that inevitable end and live a life of meaning and pleasure.

THE MEANING OF LIFE, PART II

M Y WIFE AND I spent a couple of weeks at our condo in Florida in February 2020. We go there a few times every year, especially at the tail end of winter, when we start to believe that spring will never come. Our place is in a community for people fifty-five and older. It is a quiet, clean place of two-storey condominiums with beautiful green lawns, trees, and flowers that are all taken care of by the management. The grounds are very flat and there is a canal running alongside them. In the centre lies a clubhouse and swimming pool, which is clean and warm and seems to be open all the time. The people are friendly and pretty quiet, and I assume our place is typical of these types of communities.

The pool is not far from us, and I spent a lot of time watching the snowbirds who congregated there every day to . . . well, I am not sure what. From my perspective, it looked like they did nothing at all except lie in the sun and nap.

For anyone unfamiliar with the term, a snowbird is someone who escapes the cold winter of Canada and the northern United States every year and travels to somewhere like Florida or Texas.

I do not know how often Americans travel back and forth from their winter homes to their summer ones, but Canadians are allowed (by both governments) to stay in the United States for 183 days per year. For many, it is a second home where they spend almost as much time as they do in their home country. As I said, my wife and I, since we are both still working, go for a couple of weeks at a time. However, many snowbirds head south in October or November and stay until May. That is a long time to spend every year in a temporary home.

It is such a different lifestyle than the one I am used to. I could sit by the pool for short periods of time, but not veg out the way I saw so many doing, just dozing off for long periods of time. I could not let go like that, and many of the people there were younger than me. Some just squeezed in over the minimum age restriction.

I do not mean to suggest they did absolutely nothing— although it seemed as if some did. I saw people going for walks, playing golf, shuffleboard and cards, swimming, cooking, partying, and going to the beach.

The one thing they did not do is work. They occupied their time with these activities, but often it seemed that they were just looking for something to do.

In fact, sometimes they seemed desperate for something to do. One of the results was that small things became particularly important. Once, I did not get back to the laundromat in time to catch the end of the cycle, and there was a note chastising me waiting on the machine. I had only been fifteen minutes late.

An acquaintance told me a story about visiting his parents at a high-end condo. He and his wife and children went down to the hot tub one evening and were enjoying a good soak when the security guard came and told them they had to leave. It was three minutes after ten, the guard explained, and the tub was supposed to close at 10 p.m. When my acquaintance expressed surprise that he had come down so promptly to throw them out, he pointed to all the windows that overlooked them. Several people, with nothing better to do, had been watching from just before the hour, and as soon as the clock struck the hour, they had all called the guard.

This seems to be the kind of behaviour you can expect when people in closed communities have nothing better to do and no work to occupy them.

I asked myself whether I could do that. Whether I could retire and spend six months of the year someplace warm with no work to do. I felt very conflicted. Not being productive. Not helping people. It continues to be a big question mark, but I do not think I could do it.

Yet when I talked to the people who have adopted this lifestyle and stay there for six months a year, they told me that they loved it and they really meant it. So why was I different? Was it because I had set such great store in my bucket list and have not got to the end yet? Was it because I am still on the treadmill and do not know how to get off?

I do not think so. I have given this a lot of thought. I realize that it is key for people my age to understand what "golden age" means. It is to replace things you must do with things that you want to do. Right now, in my early seventies, doing nothing is not something I want to do. That would not make me enjoy my life.

For someone else, however, a person who has toiled hard all their working life, to veg out next to the pool all day is truly an enjoyable experience. They have found their joy. It is simply different from mine.

My apparent inability to live the kind of life that others seem to enjoy goes way back. I was a dreamer as a child, and I guess that dreaming shaped my life. I am the only one of my siblings who did not follow a traditional way of life.

I have a friend who is exactly my age. We have known each other almost our entire lives. As children we were classmates and neighbours, and we have stayed in touch. He came from a large family, and at the end of grade six his father, who was an old-fashioned man, took him out of school to be apprenticed in a garage and learn car electrics. By the time he was eighteen, my friend had his own shop; he married at twenty and had his first child a year later. At that time, I was studying pedagogy at university with no thought of settling down.

When we got together, he would tell me how stupid I was to keep going to school, and I would tell him how stupid he was to live a life with such limitations. This went on for many, many years. I got my doctorate, lived in different countries, and did not marry until I was thirty-four, although, just like my friend, I had a child a year later. Whenever we got together, we had the same joking argument. Then, about ten years ago, things changed.

We were both around sixty. My friend had never moved from our hometown. He had never learned anything except the electrical system of cars. He had his shop, his food, his grandchildren, his family, and the circle of friends he grew up with. He even took the traditional nap every afternoon.

I was a professional person living in Canada with my Colombian wife and our two well-educated children. I had five university degrees, I had travelled the world, and I had met many people and done many things. Yet, seeing him, I realized that there were so many things that I missed in my life. I missed being home,

I missed being with my mother, my sisters, my brothers, and my childhood friends. I missed speaking my mother tongue. I missed Persian music. I even missed taking that nap in the afternoon.

We sat together that afternoon, drinking tea and sharing a hookah while I told him about what I had been doing and the places I had visited. He listened wide-eyed and open-mouthed, and then he turned to me, and, after all those years, he said, "I think I am the stupid one."

I realized, remembering all the things I had missed, all the things that I still miss, that he was wrong. "No," I said. "I think I am the stupid one."

So really, who was the stupid one? Maybe neither of us. We all must follow our own individual path to happiness.

Whether it is beside a swimming pool in Florida or under the blazing Persian sun, I am not ready to nap away the afternoon just yet.

BUEN CAMINO

I ONCE MET a young woman in her late twenties who decided to go for a walk. Her mother was German, and her father was African. Her parents were no longer together, and perhaps that informed her decision. Anyway, one day she left her final year of nursing school, broke up with her boyfriend of three years, shaved her head, and hit the road. She wanted to be happy but was unsure of the way. She met another young woman who was almost the same age and had a similar story. They were sweet and smart and looking for a path. I met them on the Camino de Santiago de Compostela, and when they asked me why I was there, I told them I liked walking and I liked nature.

I do not think they believed that was all there was to it.

The Camino de Santiago, or Way of Saint James, was never on my bucket list—not like climbing Mount Kilimanjaro or visiting Antarctica. But it was on my hiking buddy Pat's list. So, when he decided he would like to do the walk in 2014, I agreed to go along, and our friend Johnny decided to join us too.

Unlike the other treks we had undertaken, the Camino is long. Really long. There are a couple of routes. We decided to take the *Camino Francés*, which starts in Saint-Jean-Pied-de-Port in France and wends its way through the Pyrenees Mountains across northern Spain until it reaches its conclusion at the shrine of the apostle St. James in the Cathedral of Santiago de Compostela. It covers about eight hundred kilometres (if you do not make it longer by getting lost).

That is a lot of walking. Nonetheless, as I learned when I started researching and preparing for the trip, hundreds of thousands of people from all over the world have done it. Some have done it more than once. Some have taken several years—walking sections of it for a week or two at a time.

As part of my preparation, I learned about other people's experiences and discovered the 2010 movie *The Way*, about a man who continues the pilgrimage begun by his dead son to scatter his ashes. I found out that American actor Shirley MacLaine had walked the path and written about it in *The Camino: A Journey of the Spirit*, which I both read and listened to as an audiobook.

I also read what other people had to say about their experiences on the trail. They were all very inspirational. Several of their comments stood out:

"The thing you always wanted to do—do it."

"You are capable of more than you know."

"Spirituality is real, let it be experienced."

"Slow down, your casket will not be empty when you die."

"You do not need much."

"Appreciate the beauty and savour it."

"Give what you take."

"You may not be the fastest and that is okay."

"This, too, shall pass."

"No person is an island."

Of course, I also prepared physically. I started taking long walks daily and even longer walks on the weekend to develop my endurance. One day, I walked 36.3 kilometres from St. John's to Witless Bay (yes, that is really its name!) in about eight hours. Johnny had done the same walk a few days previously. We were just about ready.

Unfortunately (and ironically), six weeks before we were due to leave, Pat came to see me with some bad news. Because of an illness in his family, he was going to have to cancel his trip. This was sad for me and even worse for Pat, who was the instigator of the trip. What to do? Johnny was ready to go anyway, and I decided to go with him. I cannot deny, though, that if Johnny had not made that decision, I would not have gone. It would not be the same without Pat, and I would have waited for him. (Fortunately, he was able to go three years later with our other hiking buddy, Paddy.)

Johnny and I set off in the early fall of 2014. I met him in Paris, where we quickly toured around, visiting the Eiffel Tower and walking down the Champs-Élysées to the Arc de Triomphe. We arrived the next day at Saint-Jean-Pied-de-Port, got our Camino passports, and started walking the twenty-seven kilometres to Roncesvalles in Spain to become pilgrims.

Johnny has longer legs than me and soon left me behind. I had a real feeling of adventure and accomplishment when I arrived at mealtime and we met up again. That first night we stayed in a residence next to the church, where we slept in bunk beds in a large hall with 120 other people. It reminded me of my military service training back in 1970 and was a good introduction to the Camino.

We soon fell into a pattern. We would begin walking at seven or eight in the morning and arrive at our destination for the day by about four or five o'clock. As I have mentioned previously, because of those long legs, Johnny would usually pull ahead, so we had little signals he would leave on the trail to indicate what direction he had taken at a crossroads or where to meet for lunch.

One day, Johnny took a wrong turn. I was worried when I got to the *albergue*, or hostel, where we would be staying that night and discovered he had not arrived. I waited for a couple of anxious hours before seeing him stagger in from the direction opposite the one he should have been coming from. I quickly prepared a soothing foot bath for him.

Part of the Camino experience is the communality. Dinner is served at large tables where pilgrims eat together and share their days' adventures. For just a few euros, the food and wine are as plentiful as the company.

It took me about four nights to get used to the *albergues*. A large group of people sleeping makes an equally large amount of noise—groaning, moaning, and snoring in many languages, a real international cacophony I wish I could explain. *Do not process these noises*, I instructed my brain, but it took a few days before it finally listened to me.

There were other misadventures besides Johnny getting lost.

On the third day, I twisted my ankle while crossing a dry riverbed. But what seemed like a problem solved two others. To reduce the weight I had to carry, I discovered a service that would transport my backpack to the next stop every day. That was a real help. And because of the necessity of having a place to send the backpack, we had somewhere reserved every night and did not need to find a place to stay.

One day I was limping along, and a young woman came up behind me and asked why. I told her about twisting my ankle. She was a physiotherapist and insisted that I allow her to have a look at my ankle when we stopped at the next *albergue*. Later that evening, we sat in the backyard of the *albergue* surrounded by other hikers and pilgrims as she examined me. Then she massaged my foot with a medicinal ointment, and it was the best massage I ever had. What a relief. I remember her smile and satisfaction while she provided me with assistance and comfort.

She was one of many people we encountered as we walked during the day and in the thirty-five *albergues*, churches, and convents we ate and slept in at night. Sometimes we would spend a day or two with someone. Other times, it was just a brief chat or *Buen Camino*, meaning "Good Journey" or "Good Path," the universal greeting of the trek.

There were good people, weird people, and everyone in between, and they all had their own reason for the journey they were undertaking. I met a couple from France who had lost a son in an accident. They were walking to work through their grief.

Another time, I met two women who must have been at least eighty years old. They had been friends all their lives. They had lost their spouses; their children were all grown, and here they were. They managed about five or six kilometres a day and stayed as long as they liked in the small towns along the way. They expected to take about six months to complete their pilgrimage. I lunched with them one day in the middle of nowhere.

I met a very gentle middle-aged woman from the Middle East who worked as a flight attendant. She suffered from depression and hoped the walk would help. We walked together for several days, but she eventually had to give up because of leg problems.

I met another woman who was also a psychologist, who had undertaken the journey to do something different. We talked about our profession.

I met a man around my own age whose partner lived in New York. Throughout the hike, they stayed in close contact by phone. It was as if the other man were there and taking part in the journey.

Although I was not that dedicated to keeping in touch with the people back home, I liked to stop for a few minutes in any cafés or restaurants I found to use their Wi-Fi (which they called "wee fee"). I also enjoyed stopping in the churches that lined the route. I always found it a relaxing and positive experience to rest in such a place for a short while.

Despite all the people I encountered, I spent a lot of time alone as I passed farms, vineyards, apple orchards, and forests. With all that time, as I walked along undistracted, I began to question my own motivations. Why was I doing this?

I started thinking about others' experiences. Some people, especially Catholics, saw the journey as a pilgrimage. Others were trying to find themselves and their life path. I thought I was just enjoying setting a daily goal to get from point A to point B and appreciating my surroundings as I fulfilled that goal. I thought I did not really need another purpose.

The more I walked, the more I found myself reviewing my life. And as I mentioned early on in this book, I learned that I was not afraid to die. Perhaps those two young women who did not believe my motivation were right. Perhaps I, too, was on a spiritual journey. I just did not realize it at the outset.

Once upon a time, there was a man in his sixties who decided to go for a walk.

It took us thirty-four days to complete our epic hike, and it was raining the afternoon we arrived in Santiago de Compostela, where we each received a certificate to mark the successful completion of our trip.

"*Buen Camino.*"

"*Gracias.*"

ACKNOWLEDGEMENTS

Many thanks to Denise Flint, who helped me write this book, chapter by chapter. To Pamela Dooley, Leslie Vryenhoek, Helen Martinez, and Patricia Hurley for editing. A special thank you to my mentor, Herb Hopkins, who helped get this booked published.